# TURKISH MEZE

# TURKISH MEZE

## The Little Dishes of the Eastern Mediterranean

A mouthwatering collection of dips, purées, soups, salads and snacks

**Ghillie Başan**

60 recipes shown step by step in more than 300 stunning photographs

With photography by Martin Brigdale

southwater

This edition is published by Southwater,
an imprint of Anness Publishing Ltd
Hermes House, 88–89 Blackfriars Road,
London SE1 8HA;
tel. 020 7401 2077; fax 020 7633 9499

www.southwaterbooks.com; www.annesspublishing.com

If you like the images in this book and would like to investigate using
them for publishing, promotions or advertising, please visit our website
www.practicalpictures.com for more information.

UK agent: The Manning Partnership Ltd;
tel. 01225 478444; fax 01225 478440;
sales@manning-partnership.co.uk

UK distributor: Grantham Book  Services Ltd;
tel. 01476 541080; fax 01476 541061; orders@gbs.tbs-ltd.co.uk

North American agent/distributor: National Book Network;
tel. 301 459 3366; fax 301 429 5746; www.nbnbooks.com

Australian agent/distributor: Pan Macmillan Australia;
tel. 1300 135 113; fax 1300 135 103;
customer.service@macmillan.com.au

New Zealand agent/distributor: David Bateman Ltd;
tel. (09) 415 7664; fax (09) 415 8892

ETHICAL TRADING POLICY
At Anness Publishing we believe that business should be conducted in an
ethical and ecologically sustainable way, with respect for the environment
and a proper regard to the replacement of the natural resources we employ.

As a publisher, we use a lot of wood pulp to make high-quality paper
for printing, and that wood commonly comes from spruce trees. We are
therefore currently growing more than 750,000 trees in three Scottish
forest plantations: Berrymoss (130 hectares/320 acres), West Touxhill
(125 hectares/305 acres) and Deveron Forest (75 hectares/185 acres).
The forests we manage contain more than 3.5 times the number of trees
employed each year in making paper for the books we manufacture.

Because of this ongoing ecological investment programme, you, as our
customer, can have the pleasure and reassurance of knowing that a tree is
being cultivated on your behalf to naturally replace the materials used to
make the book you are holding.

Our forestry programme is run in accordance with the UK Woodland
Assurance Scheme (UKWAS) and will be certified by the internationally
recognized Forest Stewardship Council (FSC). The FSC is a non-government
organization dedicated to promoting responsible management of the
world's forests. Certification ensures forests are managed in an
environmentally sustainable and socially responsible way. For further
information about this scheme, go to www.annesspublishing.com/trees

Publisher: Joanna Lorenz
Senior Project Editors: Lucy Doncaster and Felicity Forster
Copy Editors: Jan Cutler and Jeni Wright
Designer: Nigel Partridge
Home Economists: Fergal Connolly and Sunil Vijayakar
Stylist: Helen Trent
Production Controller: Don Campaniello

© Anness Publishing Ltd 2009

Previously published as part of a larger volume,
*The Food and Cooking of Turkey*.

PUBLISHER'S NOTE

Although the advice and information in this book are believed
to be accurate and true at the time of going to press, neither
the authors nor the publisher can accept any legal responsiblity
or liability for any errors or omissions that may be made.

NOTES
Bracketed terms are intended for American readers.

For all recipes, quantities are given in both metric and imperial measures
and, where appropriate, in standard cups and spoons. Follow one set of
measures, but not a mixture, because they are not interchangeable.

Standard spoon and cup measures are level. 1 tsp = 5ml,
1 tbsp = 15ml, 1 cup = 250ml/8fl oz.

Australian standard tablespoons are 20ml. Australian readers should
use 3 tsp in place of 1 tbsp for measuring small quantities.
American pints are 16fl oz/2 cups. American readers should use
20fl oz/2.5 cups in place of 1 pint when measuring liquids.

Electric oven temperatures in this book are for conventional ovens.
When using a fan oven, the temperature will probably need to be reduced
by about 10–20°C/20–40°F. Since ovens vary, you should check with
your manufacturer's instruction book for guidance.

The nutritional analysis given for each recipe is calculated per portion
(i.e. serving or item), unless otherwise stated. If the recipe gives a range,
such as Serves 4–6, then the nutritional analysis will be for the smaller
portion size, i.e. 6 servings.

Measurements for sodium do not include salt added to taste.

Medium (US large) eggs are used unless otherwise stated.

# CONTENTS

### INTRODUCTION 6

# INTRODUCTION

Diverse, endlessly fascinating and steeped in history, Turkey combines the ancient with the contemporary, the religious with the mystical, and boasts a peaceful landscape dotted with impressive mosques, ancient Roman and Greek ruins, colourful markets, and rustic villages full of cheerful children.

Everywhere you turn in Turkey there is something delicious to eat, whether it is enjoyed outdoors as street food, in a restaurant or as part of an ancient tradition called meze. This collection of small dishes can include an amazing range of foods, from garlic-flavoured, smoked aubergine (eggplant) purée, cracked wheat salad and crushed green olives with coriander seeds to light, crisp, cigar-shaped pastries filled with white cheese, mint and dill, plump mussels coated in a beer batter and deep-fried, and a dazzling array of sweet pastries drenched in sticky syrup.

The meze table is not regulated by time or order, just the understanding that the food should be served in small quantities to be savoured at a leisurely pace, and that one should rise feeling contented and comfortable, not stuffed.

## TITBITS FOR A 'PLEASANT TASTE'

The wonderful thing about meze is that there really are no rules. Traditionally, a table of meze dishes would be laid out to accompany the alcoholic drink, rakı, with the aim of achieving a 'pleasant head', not to fill one's belly but to delight one's palate and whet the appetite in anticipation of the main meal served later. Often loosely translated as hors d'oeuvre, an appetizer or a tasty snack, the versatility of meze enables it to be all of these things and much more besides.

The literal translation of meze is a 'pleasant taste' and that is just what it is: something tasty. Some people insist that only a bowl of nuts, olives or small pieces of fresh or dried fruit constitute the true meze, whereas many others feel that almost anything and everything qualifies, from warm, freshly toasted

*Above: Simple meze – a bowl of green plums, erik, that are dipped in salt.*

pumpkin seeds to small, succulent lamb kebabs, or even some hot snacks and soups, such as flatbreads with spicy lamb and tomato or the much-loved tripe soup.

## FRUIT MEZE

For those who believe that meze should consist of just one fruit, each season offers its own gems, such as slices of fresh quince with a squeeze of lemon, the unripe, firm, tart-tasting green plums (erik) that are dipped in salt, and the large pomegranates dripping

*Below: A meze spread consisting of Smoked Aubergine with Yogurt Purée; Salad of Feta, Chillies and Parsley; Grated Beetroot and Yogurt Salad; and bread.*

### The history of meze
Dating back to the ancient Greeks, Romans and Persians, as well as medieval Arabs and Ottomans, the tradition of meze has a long history. Until relatively recently, it was a custom enjoyed by men alone – traders, travellers, noblemen, kings and sultans.

The word meze is thought to have originated from the Persian word maza, which means relish or 'taste', and is the word used in Syria and Lebanon, whereas in other parts of the Middle East the word is mezze. All these words traditionally referred to small morsels, or portions, of flavoursome food served to accompany a spirit or wine.

*Above: Marinated olives with oregano and lemon make a tasty meze dish.*

*Above: Made from puréed chickpeas mixed with sesame seed paste, garlic and lemon juice, hummus is an extremely popular ezme dish.*

with juice. Fresh watermelon, cherries, apricots and figs are also popular, but the most widespread fruit has always been a sweet, juicy melon cut into golden chunks and served on its own, or with cubes of white cheese.

## SALADS AND SIMPLE MEZE

Meze and salads go hand in hand, as many salads are served as meze and some dishes are called 'salad', even if they do not resemble one.

The most primitive form of meze is a small plate of çerez, which usually consists of a dainty serving of dried fruit, such as white mulberries, or plump olives with a squeeze of lemon juice, or even just a selection of nuts, roasted pumpkin seeds, salted sunflower seeds, or roasted chickpeas (leblebi), the traditional accompaniment to the drink, rakı. Full of protein and minerals, and delicious when freshly roasted, nuts have long been eaten as appetizers because they are reputed to increase one's toleration of alcohol.

*Right: A table bearing an array of salads and other meze dishes can be prepared for a buffet or large family gathering.*

Another simple form of meze is the popular ezme, which consists of ingredients that are beaten, crushed, mashed, pounded, puréed, or pressed into a paste. An ezme dish should be of a consistency that is perfect for scooping up with bread and, in some cases, for

treating as a dip. Not all dishes that are pounded or puréed are called ezme – some have their own names like hummus, made with chickpeas, tarama, made with fish roe, and fava, a dish of puréed broad beans; others come under the umbrella title salata (salad).

# COLD MEZE

In Turkey, there is a huge range of tantalizing cold meze on offer, from creamy dips and purées to poached vegetables and stuffed vine leaves. In these pages you will find some the most famous examples, including Hummus, Sesame and Lemon Dip, and Vine Leaves Stuffed with Aromatic Rice, as well as some less well-known treats, like Carrot and Caraway Purée with Yogurt, Fiery Cheese and Parsley Dip, and Artichokes with Beans and Almonds.

# HUMMUS

*THIS IS ONE OF THOSE DISHES THAT YOU SHOULD MAKE ACCORDING TO YOUR PERSONAL TASTE. SOME PEOPLE LIKE HUMMUS STRONGLY FLAVOURED WITH GARLIC, SOME LIKE IT THICKENED WITH SESAME PASTE, AND OTHERS PREFER IT LIGHT AND LEMONY. THIS CLASSIC TURKISH VERSION, HUMUS, IS LIGHT WITH A HINT OF CUMIN, AND IS DELICIOUS SERVED WITH WARM FLAT BREAD OR CRUDITÉS. IT IS NEARLY ALWAYS ACCOMPANIED BY A BOWL OF GREEN OLIVES OR PICKLED VEGETABLES AND CAN BE GARNISHED WITH CHOPPED PARSLEY OR SUMAC, OR WITH TOASTED PINE NUTS OR SESAME SEEDS.*

SERVES FOUR TO SIX

INGREDIENTS
   225g/8oz dried chickpeas, soaked in water for at least 6 hours
   45–60ml/3–4 tbsp olive oil
   juice of 1–2 lemons
   2 garlic cloves, crushed
   5ml/1 tsp cumin seeds
   15–30ml/1–2 tbsp thick and creamy natural (plain) yogurt
   salt and ground black pepper
To garnish:
   15ml/1 tbsp olive oil
   kırmızı biber, or paprika

**1** Drain the chickpeas and place them in a pan with plenty of water. Bring to the boil, reduce the heat and simmer, covered, for about 1½ hours, or until they are very soft. Drain the chickpeas.

**2** Remove any loose skins by rubbing the chickpeas in a clean kitchen towel. Put the cooked chickpeas into a food processor or blender and process to a thick purée.

**3** Add the olive oil, lemon juice, garlic and cumin seeds, and blend thoroughly. Add the yogurt to lighten the mixture, and season to taste. Adjust the hummus to your taste by adding a little more lemon or olive oil.

**4** Transfer the hummus to a serving bowl and drizzle a little oil over the surface to keep it moist. Sprinkle a little kırmızı biber or paprika over the top of the hummus and serve with warm bread or carrot and celery sticks.

**Per portion** Energy 190kcal/798kJ; Protein 8.4g; Carbohydrate 19.3g, of which sugars 1.4g; Fat 9.4g, of which saturates 1.3g; Cholesterol 0mg; Calcium 70mg; Fibre 4.1g; Sodium 19mg.

# SESAME AND LEMON DIP

*THIS DELIGHTFUL LITTLE DIP, TAHIN TARAMA, IS FROM CENTRAL ANATOLIA, WHERE IT IS OFTEN SERVED IN OUTDOOR CAFÉS AND RESTAURANTS AS A MEZE DISH ON ITS OWN — A SORT OF WHETTING OF THE APPETITE WHILE YOU WAIT FOR THE ASSORTMENT OF EXCITING DISHES TO COME. SOMETIMES YOU WILL SEE GROUPS OF OLD MEN DRINKING RAKI OR REFRESHING TEA, SHARING A PLATE OF TAHIN TARAMA OR A BOWL OF ROASTED CHICKPEAS WHILE THEY PLAY CARDS OR BACKGAMMON. SWEET AND TANGY, IT IS GOOD MOPPED UP WITH CHUNKS OF CRUSTY BREAD OR TOASTED PITTA BREAD.*

SERVES TWO

INGREDIENTS
  45ml/3 tbsp light sesame paste (tahini)
  juice of 1 lemon
  15–30ml/1–2 tbsp clear honey or
    grape pekmez
  5–10ml/1–2 tsp dried mint
  lemon wedges, to serve

**VARIATION**
Popular for breakfast or as a sweet snack is tahin pekmez. Combine 30–45ml/ 2–3 tbsp light sesame paste with 30ml/ 2 tbsp grape pekmez to form a sweet paste, then scoop up with chunks of fresh bread. If you can't find pekmez, use date syrup from Middle Eastern and health food stores.

**1** Beat the sesame paste and lemon juice together in a bowl.

**2** Add the honey and mint and beat again until thick and creamy, then spoon into a small dish. Serve the dip at room temperature, with lemon wedges for squeezing.

**Per portion** Energy 160kcal/664kJ; Protein 4.3g; Carbohydrate 6.4g, of which sugars 6.2g; Fat 13.3g, of which saturates 1.9g; Cholesterol 0mg; Calcium 155mg; Fibre 1.8g; Sodium 6mg.

# SMOKED AUBERGINE AND YOGURT PURÉE

*ONE OF THE MOST POPULAR MEZE DISHES, THIS GARLIC-FLAVOURED PURÉE, PATLICAN EZMESI, VARIES FROM HOUSE TO HOUSE AND REGION TO REGION, SOMETIMES MADE WITH A ROBUST QUANTITY OF GARLIC OR A KICK OF CHILLI, OR WITH THE ADDITION OF FRESH-TASTING DILL, MINT OR PARSLEY. IT IS HEAVENLY WHEN FRESHLY MADE, SERVED WITH CHUNKS OF CRUSTY BREAD FOR SCOOPING.*

**3** Hold each aubergine by the stalk under cold running water and peel off the charred skin until you are left with just the flesh. Squeeze the flesh to get rid of any excess water and place it on a chopping board.

**4** Chop the aubergine flesh to a pulp, discarding the stalks. Put in a bowl with 30ml/2 tbsp oil, the lemon juice and garlic. Beat well to mix, then beat in the yogurt and season with salt and pepper.

**5** Transfer to a small bowl, drizzle with olive oil and garnish with dill. Serve at room temperature, with lemon wedges for squeezing.

**COOK'S TIP**
This is a great dish for a barbecue. Instead of charring the aubergines on the stove, lay them on the rack over hot charcoal and cook for 15–20 minutes, turning them from time to time until they are soft. Place them on a chopping board and slit open lengthways with a sharp knife. Scoop out the flesh and chop to a pulp, then continue as above.

## SERVES FOUR

### INGREDIENTS
2 large, plump aubergines (eggplants)
30ml/2 tbsp olive oil, plus extra for drizzling
juice of 1 lemon
2–3 garlic cloves, crushed
225g/8oz/1 cup thick and creamy natural (plain) yogurt
salt and ground black pepper
a few fresh dill fronds, to garnish
lemon wedges, to serve

### VARIATION
To make an aubergine (eggplant) salad (patlıcan salatası), toss the smoked aubergine flesh with the oil and lemon juice, some sliced spring onions (scallions), chopped tomatoes, parsley and dill.

**1** Gripping them firmly between tongs, place the aubergines directly on the gas flame on top of the stove, or under a conventional grill (broiler), and turn them from time to time until the skin is charred on all sides and the flesh feels soft to the touch.

**2** Place the aubergines in a plastic bag and leave for a few minutes.

**Per portion** Energy 103kcal/431kJ; Protein 4.4g; Carbohydrate 7.7g, of which sugars 6.4g; Fat 6.5g, of which saturates 1.2g; Cholesterol 1mg; Calcium 118mg; Fibre 2.3g; Sodium 49mg.

# CARROT AND CARAWAY PURÉE WITH YOGURT

*LONG, THIN CARROTS THAT ARE ORANGE, YELLOW, RED AND PURPLE ARE A COLOURFUL FEATURE IN THE VEGETABLE MARKETS THROUGHOUT TURKEY. USED MAINLY IN SALADS, LENTIL DISHES AND STEWS, THEY ARE ALSO STEAMED AND PURÉED, THEN SERVED WITH YOGURT IN THE MIDDLE, AS IN THIS RECIPE. TRY SERVING THE CARROT PURÉE WHILE IT IS STILL WARM, WITH CHUNKS OF CRUSTY BREAD.*

SERVES FOUR

INGREDIENTS
    6 large carrots, thickly sliced
    5ml/1 tsp caraway seeds
    30–45ml/2–3 tbsp olive oil
    juice of 1 lemon
    225g/8oz/1 cup thick and creamy
      natural (plain) yogurt
    1–2 garlic cloves, crushed
    salt and ground black pepper
    a few fresh mint leaves, to garnish

**COOK'S TIP**
It is always best to steam rather than boil vegetables, so they retain their taste, texture and goodness. This purée would not taste nearly as good if the carrots were boiled and watery.

**1** Steam the carrots for 25 minutes, until they are very soft. While they are still warm, mash them to a smooth purée, or blend them in a processor.

**2** Beat the caraway seeds into the carrot purée, followed by the oil and lemon juice. Season with salt and pepper.

**3** Beat the yogurt and garlic in a separate bowl, and season to taste.

**4** Spoon the warm carrot purée around the edge of a serving dish, or pile into a mound and make a well in the middle. Spoon the yogurt into the middle, and garnish with mint.

**Per portion** Energy 157kcal/651kJ; Protein 4.2g; Carbohydrate 15.3g, of which sugars 13.6g; Fat 9.2g, of which saturates 1.6g; Cholesterol 1mg; Calcium 140mg; Fibre 3.3g; Sodium 78mg.

# FIERY CHEESE AND PARSLEY DIP

*THIS MEZE DISH, PAŞA EZMESI, IS FIT FOR A PAŞA (A TURKISH NOBLEMAN). A REGULAR FEATURE ON THE MEZE TABLE OF CENTRAL ANATOLIA, IT IS SPIKED WITH KIRMIZI BIBER AND USED TO WHET THE APPETITE FOR THE DISHES TO FOLLOW. AS IT CAN BE VERY HOT, IT IS OFTEN SERVED WITH TAHINLI TARAMA, A SWEET MEZE DISH OF SESAME PASTE, GRAPE SYRUP AND MINT, OR KAYMAK BAL, CLOTTED BUFFALO CREAM DRIZZLED IN HONEY, TO CUT THE SPICE. SERVE WITH WARM FLAT BREAD.*

SERVES THREE TO FOUR

INGREDIENTS

    250g/9oz beyaz peynir,
      or feta cheese
    15–30ml/1–2 tbsp süzme,
      or strained yogurt
    5–10ml/1–2 tsp kırmızı biber,
      or hot paprika or chilli powder
    1 small bunch flat leaf parsley,
      leaves finely chopped
    salt, to taste
    1 lemon, cut into wedges and
      1 small bunch flat leaf parsley,
      trimmed, to serve

**1** In a bowl, mash the cheese with a fork, or process it in a food processor or blender. Beat in the yogurt, again using the fork or the blender, until the mixture is fairly smooth and creamy.

**2** Add the kırmızı biber and the parsley. Taste the dip to see if you need to add any salt – often the cheese is sufficiently salty.

**3** Spoon the cheese dip into a dish and serve as part of a meze spread with warm flat bread, such as pitta pouches or Turkish pide, wedges of lemon to squeeze over each mouthful and leafy stalks of flat leaf parsley to chew on, to cut the spice.

**VARIATIONS**
• Crushed walnuts can be mixed in to the dip in step 2, or sprinkled over the top, to add some texture to the dip.
• Finely chopped fresh mint can be added to the parsley to give a refreshing lift to the dish.

Per portion Energy 170kcal/705kJ; Protein 10.7g; Carbohydrate 2.4g, of which sugars 1.5g; Fat 13.2g, of which saturates 8.6g; Cholesterol 44mg; Calcium 262mg; Fibre 0.6g; Sodium 908mg.

# BROAD BEAN PURÉE

*THIS DELICIOUS BROAD BEAN PURÉE IS A TRADITIONAL DISH THAT IS MADE WHEN THE BEANS ARE IN SEASON. AN ACQUIRED TASTE, FAVA IS PARTICULARLY SOUGHT AFTER IN ISTANBUL, WHERE IT IS ALWAYS SERVED COLD AS A MEZE DISH. IT IS MADE WITH LARGE QUANTITIES OF OLIVE OIL FOR TASTE AND FOR THE DESIRED SMOOTH AND SILKY CONSISTENCY. IT IS OFTEN GARNISHED WITH CHUNKS OF JUICY TOMATO AND DELICATE FRONDS OF DILL, MAKING A VERY ATTRACTIVE DISH.*

### SERVES FOUR

INGREDIENTS
  225g/8oz/1¼ cups dried broad
    (fava) beans, soaked overnight
  175g/6oz fresh broad (fava)
    beans, shelled
  550ml/18fl oz/2½ cups water
  1 onion, chopped
  1 potato, peeled and chopped
  150ml/¼ pint/⅔ cup olive oil
  5ml/1 tsp salt
  10ml/2 tsp sugar
For the garnish
  1 tomato
  a few dill fronds

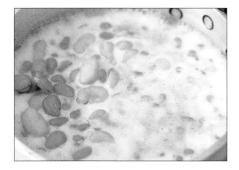

**1** Put the dried and fresh beans into a pan with the water and bring to the boil. Add the onion and potato and reduce the heat.

**2** Pour in the oil and sprinkle the salt and sugar over the top. Cover and simmer for 1 hour, stirring occasionally and topping up the water if necessary, until the purée has a pouring consistency.

**3** Press the purée through a sieve (strainer), or process it in food processor or blender. Pour it into a wet mould or bowl. Leave to cool and set.

**4** To make the garnish, plunge the tomato into a bowl of boiling water for 30 seconds, then refresh in cold water. Peel away the skin. Remove and discard the seeds and finely chop the flesh.

**5** Invert the mould or bowl on to a serving plate and garnish the purée with a cluster of chopped tomato on the very top with the dill feathers sprinkled about.

**6** Serve at room temperature with other meze dishes.

**Per portion** Energy 465kcal/1944kJ; Protein 17g; Carbohydrate 42.8g, of which sugars 6.2g; Fat 26.2g, of which saturates 3.8g; Cholesterol 0mg; Calcium 89mg; Fibre 12.5g; Sodium 21mg.

# SMOKED AUBERGINE AND PEPPER DIP

*THIS IS A LOVELY ANATOLIAN MEZE DISH OF SMOKED AUBERGINE AND PEPPERS WITH A REFRESHING LEMONY TANG. ARABIC IN ORIGIN, ACVAR IS TRADITIONALLY SERVED WARM WITH LEMON WEDGES TO SQUEEZE OVER IT. ALTERNATIVELY, YOU CAN INCREASE THE QUANTITIES AND SERVE IT AS A MAIN DISH WITH YOGURT AND BREAD, OR SERVE IT AS AN ACCOMPANIMENT TO A BARBECUE SPREAD.*

**2** One at a time, hold the charred vegetables under cold running water and peel off the skins.

**3** Place them on a chopping board and remove the stalks. Halve the peppers lengthways and scoop out the seeds, then chop the flesh to a pulp. Chop the aubergine flesh to a pulp.

**4** Pour the oil into a wide, heavy pan and toss in the onion, chilli, garlic and sugar. Cook over a medium heat for 2–3 minutes, until they begin to colour.

**5** Toss in the pulped peppers and aubergine, stir in the lemon juice and vinegar and season to taste with salt and pepper. Toss in the parsley and serve with lemon wedges and toasted pitta bread.

## SERVES FOUR

INGREDIENTS
  2 red (bell) peppers
  1 fat aubergine (eggplant)
  30–45ml/2–3 tbsp olive oil
  1 red onion, cut in half lengthways
    and finely sliced along the grain
  1 fresh red chilli, seeded and
    finely sliced
  2 garlic cloves, chopped
  5–10ml/1–2 tsp sugar
  juice of 1 lemon
  dash of white wine vinegar
  a big handful of fresh flat leaf
    parsley, roughly chopped
  salt and ground black pepper
  lemon wedges and toasted pitta
    bread, to serve

**1** Place the peppers and aubergine directly on the gas flame on top of the stove, under a conventional grill (broiler), or on a rack over the hot coals of a barbecue. Turn from time to time until the skin is charred on all sides and the flesh feels soft. Place in a plastic bag and leave for a few minutes.

**Per portion** Energy 102kcal/425kJ; Protein 1.8g; Carbohydrate 10.5g, of which sugars 9.8g; Fat 6.2g, of which saturates 1g; Cholesterol 0mg; Calcium 19mg; Fibre 3.1g; Sodium 6mg.

# SMOKED COD'S ROE DIP

*TRADITIONALLY, THIS DISH IS MADE WITH THE SMOKED ROE (TARAMA) OF GREY MULLET, ALTHOUGH THE ROE OF OTHER FISH CAN BE USED, AND THE MOST EASILY AVAILABLE IS SMOKED COD'S ROE. LIKE HUMUS, TARAMA NEEDS TO BE MADE ACCORDING TO TASTE, ADJUSTING THE OIL AND LEMON AND THE DENSITY OF THE PURÉE. WARM BREAD AND STRIPS OF CUCUMBER ARE IDEAL ACCOMPANIMENTS.*

SERVES FOUR TO SIX

INGREDIENTS
  2 slices white bread, with the
    crusts removed
  about 105ml/7 tbsp milk or water
  225g/8oz smoked cod's roe,
    skin removed
  2–3 garlic cloves, crushed
  45–60ml/3–4 tbsp olive oil, or a
    mixture of olive and sunflower oil
  juice of 2 lemons
  salt and ground black pepper
  finely chopped flat leaf parsley,
    to garnish

**2** Using a mortar and pestle, pound the roe to a smooth paste. Add the bread and garlic, and gradually pour in the olive oil and lemon juice, until the purée is creamy – adjust the quantity of oil and lemon juice to your taste.

**3** Season the purée with salt and a generous grinding of black pepper, and transfer it to a serving bowl.

**4** Garnish the dip with a little chopped parsley and serve with warm bread and strips of cucumber sprinkled with salt.

**VARIATION**
Some cooks in Turkey prefer to make a delicious warm version of tarama by using mashed potato instead of the soaked bread. Simply mix the smoked roe with freshly made hot mashed potato and garnish it with chopped parsley. Using this method makes the purée a little heavier when left to stand.

**1** First soak the bread in a bowl with a little milk or water (the quantity will vary according to the size and type of bread). Squeeze the bread to remove the excess liquid.

**Per portion** Energy 118kcal/495kJ; Protein 9.6g; Carbohydrate 5.1g, of which sugars 1.2g; Fat 6.8g, of which saturates 1.1g; Cholesterol 125mg; Calcium 48mg; Fibre 0.5g; Sodium 94mg.

# ARTICHOKES <u>WITH</u> BEANS <u>AND</u> ALMONDS

*IN THE EARLY SUMMER, MARKETS AND STREET-SELLERS DISPLAY CRATES OF GLOBE ARTICHOKES, WHICH THE TURKS LOVE TO POACH IN OLIVE OIL. OFTEN THE SELLER WILL HAVE THEM PREPARED READY FOR POACHING, OR WILL DO IT WHILE YOU WAIT. THE TENDER BOTTOMS ARE TRADITIONALLY FILLED WITH FRESH BROAD BEANS AND FLAVOURED WITH DILL, BUT SOMETIMES DICED CARROTS, POTATOES, WHOLE BABY SHALLOTS AND FRESH PEAS ARE USED AS A FILLING, OR THE POACHED ARTICHOKES ARE SIMPLY SERVED BY THEMSELVES WITH A LITTLE DILL. READY-PREPARED ARTICHOKE BOTTOMS ARE AVAILABLE FROZEN IN SOME SUPERMARKETS AND MIDDLE EASTERN STORES, OTHERWISE FOLLOW THE PREPARATION BELOW. SERVE AS AN APPETIZER OR AS A SIDE DISH.*

### SERVES FOUR

INGREDIENTS
  4 large globe artichokes
  175g/6oz/2 cups broad (fava) beans
  120ml/4fl oz/½ cup olive oil
  juice of 1 lemon
  10ml/2 tsp granulated sugar
  75g/3oz/¾ cup blanched almonds
  1 small bunch of fresh dill, chopped
  2 tomatoes, skinned, seeded
    and diced
  salt

**1** To prepare the artichokes, cut off the stalks and pull off all the leaves. Dig out the hairy choke from the middle with a spoon, then cut away any hard bits with a sharp knife and trim into a neat cup shape. Rub the cups – called bottoms – with a mixture of lemon juice and salt to prevent them from discolouring.

**COOK'S TIPS**
• Until ready to use, fresh artichokes should be treated like flowers and put in a jug (pitcher) of water.
• Buy fresh-looking almonds in their skins. Put them in a bowl and cover with boiling water. Leave to soak for a few hours until the skins loosen, then rub the skins off with your fingers. If you leave them for as long as 24 hours, the nuts soften, too.

**2** To prepare the beans, split them down the seam at the side using your thumb nail, then push out the beans with the pad of your thumb.

**3** Put the beans in large pan of water and bring to the boil. Lower the heat and simmer for 10–15 minutes or until tender. Drain and refresh under cold running water, then peel off the skins.

**4** Place the artichokes in a heavy pan. Mix together the oil, lemon juice and 50ml/2fl oz/¼ cup water and pour over the artichokes.

**5** Cover the pan and poach the artichokes gently for about 20 minutes, then add the sugar, beans and almonds. Cover again and continue to poach gently for a further 10 minutes, or until the artichokes are tender.

**6** Toss in half the dill, season with salt, and turn off the heat. Leave the artichokes to cool in the pan.

**7** Lift the artichokes out of the pan and place them hollow-side up in a serving dish. Mix the tomatoes with the beans and almonds, spoon into the middle of the artichokes and around them, and garnish with the remaining dill. Serve at room temperature.

**Per portion** Energy 351kcal/1455kJ; Protein 8.2g; Carbohydrate 13.4g, of which sugars 8.3g; Fat 29.8g, of which saturates 3.6g; Cholesterol 0mg; Calcium 110mg; Fibre 5.5g; Sodium 29mg.

# STUFFED POACHED AUBERGINES

*WHETHER THE IMAM FAINTED FROM SHOCK OR PLEASURE AT THE QUANTITY OF OLIVE OIL USED IN THIS DISH, NO ONE KNOWS, BUT 'THE IMAM FAINTED' IS THE TRANSLATION OF IMAM BAYILDI. THE AUBERGINES ARE SOMETIMES BAKED, BUT THE MORE TRADITIONAL METHOD IS GENTLE POACHING ON TOP OF THE STOVE — WHEN COOKED THIS WAY THEY MELT IN THE MOUTH. SERVE THESE COLOURFUL STUFFED VEGETABLES AS A MEZE DISH OR WITH A GREEN SALAD FOR LUNCH OR SUPPER.*

SERVES FOUR

### INGREDIENTS

2 large aubergines (eggplants)
sunflower oil, for shallow frying
1 bunch each of fresh flat leaf
  parsley and dill
1 large onion, halved and
  finely sliced
3 tomatoes, skinned and
  finely chopped
2–3 garlic cloves,
  finely chopped
5ml/1 tsp salt
150ml/¼ pint/⅔ cup olive oil
juice of ½ lemon
15ml/1 tbsp sugar
lemon wedges, to serve

**1** Using a vegetable peeler or a small, sharp knife, peel the aubergines lengthways in stripes like a zebra.

**2** Place the aubergines in a bowl of salted water and leave for 5 minutes, then drain and pat dry.

### VARIATION

Follow steps 1–6, then place the filled aubergines (eggplants) in an ovenproof dish. Drizzle the remaining olive oil and lemon juice over the top, cover with foil and bake in the oven for about 45 minutes at 180°C/350°F/Gas 4. Remove the foil, sprinkle a little grated Parmesan cheese over the top and return to the oven for about 15 minutes, until the aubergines are browned. Serve hot.

**3** Heat about 1cm/½in sunflower oil in a wok or deep-sided pan. Place the aubergines in the oil and fry quickly on all sides to soften them. This should take a total of 3–5 minutes.

**4** Lift the aubergines out on to a chopping board and slit them open lengthways to create pockets, keeping the bottoms and both ends intact so they look like canoes when stuffed.

**5** Reserve a few dill fronds and parsley leaves for the garnish, then chop the rest and mix them in a large bowl with the onion, tomatoes and garlic. Add the salt and a little of the olive oil.

**6** Spoon the mixture into the aubergine pockets, packing it in tightly so that all of it is used up.

### COOK'S TIP

Courgettes (zucchini) are often cooked in a similar way. First, they are cut in half and deseeded, then the filling is piled into the hollow and they are baked in the oven.

**7** Place the filled aubergines side by side in a deep, heavy pan. Mix the remaining olive oil with 50ml/2fl oz/ ¼ cup water and the lemon juice, pour it over the aubergines, and sprinkle the sugar over the top.

**8** Cover the pan with a lid and place over a medium heat to get the oil hot and create some steam. Once the oil is hot, lower the heat and cook the aubergines very gently for about 1 hour, basting from time to time. They should be soft and tender, with only a little oil left in the bottom of the pan.

**9** Leave the aubergines to cool in the pan, then carefully transfer them to a serving dish and spoon the oil from the bottom of the pan over them. Garnish with the reserved dill and parsley and serve at room temperature, with lemon wedges for squeezing.

**Per portion** Energy 407kcal/1680kJ; Protein 3g; Carbohydrate 16.7g, of which sugars 14.1g; Fat 37g, of which saturates 5.1g; Cholesterol 0mg; Calcium 67mg; Fibre 4.8g; Sodium 507mg.

# VINE LEAVES STUFFED WITH AROMATIC RICE

*Devised by the Ottomans, these stuffed vine leaves, yalanci yaprak dolmasi, are a popular meze dish throughout the Middle East. They are called yalanci, which means 'false', because they contain no meat. This term applies to all vegetables that are stuffed solely with aromatic rice and then cooked in olive oil and served cold on their own or as part of a meze spread. Fresh vine leaves are readily available in some Middle Eastern and Greek markets and stores; otherwise, use the packs or jars of vine leaves preserved in brine that can be found in many large supermarkets.*

## SERVES SIX

### INGREDIENTS
24–30 fresh or preserved vine leaves, plus extra for lining the pan
45ml/3 tbsp olive oil
2 onions, finely chopped
2–3 garlic cloves, finely chopped
30ml/2 tbsp pine nuts
5ml/1 tsp ground allspice
5ml/1 tsp ground cinnamon
10–15ml/2–3 tsp sugar
225g/8oz/generous 1 cup short grain rice, well rinsed and drained
1 small bunch each of fresh parsley, mint and dill, leaves finely chopped
150ml/¼ pint/⅔ cup olive oil
150ml/¼ pint/⅔ cup water
juice of 1 lemon
salt and ground black pepper
2 lemons, thickly sliced, to serve

**1** Prepare the vine leaves (*see* Cook's Tip) and drain thoroughly. Stack them on a plate, cover with a clean dish towel to keep them moist, and set aside.

**2** Heat the oil in a heavy pan and stir in the onions and garlic. Cook until they begin to colour. Stir in the pine nuts, spices and 10ml/2 tsp sugar. Cook, stirring, for 1 minute.

**3** Add the rice, mix well, and season with salt and pepper.

**4** Pour in enough water (about 450ml/¾ pint/scant 2 cups) to just cover the rice and bring it to the boil. Reduce the heat and simmer for 10 minutes, or until all the water has been absorbed. The rice should have a bite to it. Toss in the herbs and leave the rice to cool.

**5** Place a vine leaf on a board and put a heaped teaspoon of rice at the base. Fold the stem edge over the filling, then bring both of the side edges in towards the middle of the leaf, so that the filling is sealed in. Now roll the leaf up like a small, fat cigar. Place in the palm of your hand and squeeze it lightly. Repeat with the remaining leaves and rice.

**6** In a small bowl, mix together the olive oil, water, lemon juice and remaining sugar. Line the base of a shallow pan with the extra vine leaves, then place the stuffed vine leaves on top, tightly packed side by side.

**7** Pour the olive oil mixture over the stuffed vine leaves and place a plate on top of them to prevent them from unravelling during cooking.

**8** Cover the pan and simmer gently for about 1 hour, topping up the cooking liquid if necessary. Leave the stuffed vine leaves to cool in the pan, then lift them out and arrange on a plate with slices of lemon to squeeze over them.

### COOK'S TIPS
• **Fresh leaves** Bring a pan of water to the boil and plunge the fresh leaves into it for 1–2 minutes. Drain and refresh under cold running water, then drain thoroughly. Trim off the stems, and keep covered in the refrigerator for 2–3 days.
• **Preserved leaves** Place the preserved leaves in a bowl and cover with boiling water. Soak for 15–20 minutes, using a fork to separate the leaves. Drain and return to the bowl with cold water. Soak for 2–3 minutes, then drain thoroughly.

**Per portion** Energy 411kcal/1702kJ; Protein 5g; Carbohydrate 39g, of which sugars 7.5g; Fat 26.1g, of which saturates 3.4g; Cholesterol 0mg; Calcium 58mg; Fibre 2.2g; Sodium 7mg.

# VINE LEAVES STUFFED WITH LAMB AND RICE

*VINE LEAVES ARE GENERALLY USED FOR WRAPPING AROUND FISH OR CHEESE, OR FOR STUFFING AND ROLLING INTO LOGS. THE BEST-KNOWN STUFFED VINE LEAVES ARE THE ONES FILLED WITH AROMATIC RICE AND SERVED COLD AS PART OF A MEZE SPREAD. IN TURKISH, THESE ARE KNOWN AS YALANCI YAPRAK DOLMASI, MEANING 'FALSE STUFFED VINE LEAVES', BECAUSE THEY DO NOT CONTAIN MEAT. THE MEAT-FILLED VERSION, ETLI YAPRAK DOLMASI, IS REGARDED AS THE REAL THING, AND IS USUALLY SERVED HOT AS A MAIN COURSE WITH A DOLLOP OF NATURAL YOGURT.*

## SERVES FOUR TO SIX

### INGREDIENTS
25–30 fresh or preserved vine leaves
350g/12oz/1½ cups finely minced
   (ground) lean lamb or beef
2 onions, finely chopped
115g/4oz/generous ½ cup long grain
   rice, thoroughly rinsed and drained
1 bunch each of fresh dill, flat leaf
   parsley and mint, finely chopped
45–60ml/3–4 tbsp olive oil
juice of 1 lemon
salt and ground black pepper

To serve
60–90ml/4–6 tbsp thick and creamy
   natural (plain) yogurt
1 lemon, cut into wedges

**1** If using fresh vine leaves, bring a pan of water to the boil and plunge the fresh leaves into it for 1–2 minutes. Drain and refresh under cold running water, then drain thoroughly. Trim off the stems, and keep covered in the refrigerator for 2–3 days. If using preserved leaves, place them in a bowl and cover with boiling water. Soak for 15–20 minutes, using a fork to separate the leaves. Drain and return to the bowl with cold water. Soak for 2–3 minutes, then drain thoroughly.

**VARIATION**
You can make the same dolma using the leaves of a red or green cabbage.

**2** Put the lamb in a bowl and stir in the onions, rice and herbs. Season, bind with 15ml/1 tbsp of the oil and knead.

**3** Lay one of the vine leaves on a flat surface and spoon some filling at the top of the leaf. Pull this over the filling, fold in the sides, then roll into a tight log. Repeat with the remaining leaves and filling.

**4** Arrange the vine leaves, seam side down, in a deep, wide pan. Pack them together in circles, making more than one layer if necessary.

**5** In a bowl, mix the remaining oil with the lemon juice and 150ml/¼ pint/ ⅔ cup water, then pour over the vine leaves. The liquid should come at least halfway up the top layer, so you may need to add extra liquid.

**6** Put the pan over a medium heat. Once the liquid begins to bubble, place a plate over the leaves to stop them from unravelling, followed by a lid or foil.

**7** Lower the heat and leave the vine leaves to steam gently for 45 minutes, until the rice and meat are cooked. Serve hot, with the yogurt and lemon wedges to squeeze over.

**Per portion** Energy 276kcal/1148kJ; Protein 14.6g; Carbohydrate 23.5g, of which sugars 6.6g; Fat 13.8g, of which saturates 4.4g; Cholesterol 45mg; Calcium 88mg; Fibre 2.8g; Sodium 51mg.

# SALADS

*In Turkey meze and salads go hand in hand, as many salads are served as meze and other dishes are called 'salad', even if they do not resemble one. The dishes in this chapter range from warm or cold vegetable salads served with dressings, like Grated Beetroot and Yogurt Salad, or Lamb's Lettuce Salad, to more substantial combinations made with grains or pulses, like Bulgur Salad or Bean Salad. Others are served with cheese or include fruit, such as Orange and Onion Salad with Olives.*

# LAMB'S LETTUCE SALAD

*THE LAMB'S LETTUCE IN TURKEY IS A SLIGHTLY THICKER VERSION OF THE PLANT THAN IS GENERALLY AVAILABLE ELSEWHERE. USUALLY, THE FRESH LEAVES ARE PICKED FOR THIS SUMMER SALAD, CALLED SEMIZ OTU SALATASI, WHICH IS SERVED AS PART OF A MEZE SPREAD, OR THEY ARE COOKED WITH MINCED MEAT AS PART OF A MORE SUBSTANTIAL DISH. EXTREMELY QUICK AND EASY, THIS SIMPLE SALAD IS ALSO DELICIOUS WITH GRILLED AND ROASTED MEATS AND POULTRY.*

**COOK'S TIP**
There is no rule regarding the ratio of yogurt to lamb's lettuce, as some households enjoy this salad packed with leaves, whereas others like it with double the amount of yogurt. Experiment with different ratios and make it according to your personal preference. If you do not like garlic, you could use just ¼ clove or omit it altogether.

SERVES FOUR

INGREDIENTS
about 500g/1¼lb thick and creamy
  natural (plain) yogurt
juice of 1 lemon
1–2 garlic cloves, crushed
225g/8oz fresh lamb's lettuce,
  well rinsed and drained
salt and ground black pepper

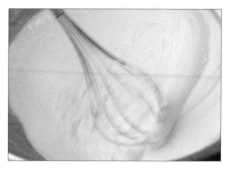

**1** In a wide bowl, beat the yogurt with the lemon juice and garlic. Season to taste with salt and pepper.

**2** Toss the lamb's lettuce into the dressing, making sure it is thoroughly coated with the yogurt.

**3** Transfer the salad to a serving bowl and serve immediately while the leaves are still fresh as a meze dish or as a salad with savoury pastries, or with grilled (broiled) and roasted meats.

**Per portion** Energy 78kcal/328kJ; Protein 6.8g; Carbohydrate 10.3g, of which sugars 10.3g; Fat 1.5g, of which saturates 0.7g; Cholesterol 2mg; Calcium 253mg; Fibre 0.5g; Sodium 106mg.

# CUCUMBER AND MINT SALAD

*REFRESHING AND VERSATILE, CACIK CAN BE SERVED AS A SALAD OR AS AN ACCOMPANIMENT. SOME FASHIONABLE RESTAURANTS IN ISTANBUL ALSO SERVE IT AS A COLD SOUP WITH CUBES OF ICE IN IT, TO BE EATEN THROUGHOUT THE MEAL. FOR THE SALAD, THE YOGURT IS KEPT THICK, WHEREAS IF SERVED AS A SOUP IT NEEDS TO BE DILUTED WITH WATER. IT CAN BE FLAVOURED WITH FRESH OR DRIED MINT, OR WITH FRESH DILL, AND THE SALAD IS OFTEN SERVED WITH OLIVE OIL ON THE TOP.*

SERVES FOUR

INGREDIENTS
  1 large cucumber or 2 small ones
  500g/1¼lb thick and creamy
    natural (plain) yogurt
  2 garlic cloves, crushed
  1 bunch fresh mint, leaves chopped
  olive oil, for drizzling
  salt and ground black pepper

**1** Using a vegetable peeler, partially peel the cucumber skin in stripes. Cut the cucumber in half lengthways and slice it finely.

**2** Place the slices in a colander and sprinkle with salt. Leave to weep for 5–10 minutes. Rinse the sliced cucumber and drain well.

**COOK'S TIP**
In kebab houses, cakic is often served as a cooling accompaniment to spicy kebabs. As a meze dish, you can slice, dice or grate the cucumber, depending on your personal preference.

**3** In a wide bowl, beat the yogurt with the garlic and most of the mint. Add the sliced cucumber and season to taste.

**4** Transfer to a serving bowl, drizzle a little olive oil over the top and garnish with the remaining chopped mint.

**5** Serve with chunks of fresh bread and other meze dishes.

**Per portion** Energy 83kcal/348kJ; Protein 7.4g; Carbohydrate 11.2g, of which sugars 10.1g; Fat 1.4g, of which saturates 0.6g; Cholesterol 2mg; Calcium 273mg; Fibre 0.4g; Sodium 107mg.

# CELERY AND COCONUT SALAD WITH LIME

*THIS SALAD IS UNUSUAL FOR TURKEY IN ITS USE OF GRATED COCONUT, WHICH IS MAINLY RESERVED AS A GARNISH FOR SWEET DISHES, OR SERVED WITH SHELLED POMEGRANATE SEEDS AS A MEDIEVAL MEZE. JUICY AND REFRESHING, THIS SALAD IS WELCOME ON A HOT SUNNY DAY AS PART OF A BUFFET SPREAD OUTDOORS, OR AS AN ACCOMPANIMENT TO GRILLED, BROILED OR BARBECUED MEATS AND SPICY DISHES. IT LOOKS ESPECIALLY APPEALING SERVED IN COCONUT SHELL HALVES.*

### SERVES THREE TO FOUR

#### INGREDIENTS
45–60ml/3–4 tbsp thick and creamy
  natural (plain) yogurt
2 garlic cloves, crushed
5ml/1 tsp grated lime zest
juice of 1 lime
8 long celery sticks, grated (leaves
  reserved for the garnish)
flesh of ½ fresh coconut, grated
salt and ground black pepper
a few sprigs of fresh flat leaf parsley,
  to garnish

**1** Mix the yogurt and garlic in a bowl, add the lime rind and juice and season with salt and pepper.

**2** Fold in the celery and coconut. Set aside for 20 minutes, then spoon into a bowl and garnish with celery and parsley.

**Per portion** Energy 126kcal/521kJ; Protein 2.1g; Carbohydrate 2.9g, of which sugars 2.9g; Fat 11.9g, of which saturates 10.1g; Cholesterol 0mg; Calcium 63mg; Fibre 3.6g; Sodium 69mg.

# GRATED BEETROOT AND YOGURT SALAD

*WITH ITS BENEFICIAL NUTRITIONAL PROPERTIES, YOGURT IS USED FREQUENTLY IN MEZE DISHES. IT IS EVEN SERVED ON ITS OWN, DRIZZLED WITH A LITTLE HONEY, OR SPRINKLED WITH ICING SUGAR. THE MOST FAMOUS OF THE YOGURT DIPS IS SMOKED AUBERGINE AND YOGURT PURÉE, BUT THERE ARE A FEW OTHER GEMS THAT GET LITTLE MENTION, SUCH AS THIS ONE MADE WITH GRATED BEETROOT. SPIKED WITH GARLIC AND A PRETTY SHADE OF PINK, IT IS DELICIOUS SCOOPED ON TO FLAT BREAD.*

SERVES FOUR

INGREDIENTS
4 raw beetroot (beets), washed
  and trimmed
500g/1¼lb/2¼ cups thick and
  creamy natural (plain) yogurt
2 garlic cloves, crushed
salt and ground black pepper
a few fresh mint leaves, shredded,
  to garnish

**1** Boil the beetroot in plenty of water for 35–40 minutes until tender, but not soft or mushy. Drain and refresh under cold running water.

**VARIATIONS**
• To make a carrot version of this salad, cut four carrots into chunks and steam them for about 15 minutes, until they are tender but still retain some bite. Leave the carrot chunks until they are cool enough to handle, then grate and mix with the yogurt and garlic. Season to taste with salt and pepper and garnish with mint or dill.
• In some households, the beetroot (beet) is diced and stir-fried with coriander seeds, sugar and a splash of apple vinegar. Then it is served warm with the cooling garlic-flavoured yogurt and garnished with dill.

**2** Peel off the skins and grate the beetroot on to a plate. Squeeze it with your fingers to drain off excess water.

**3** In a bowl, beat the yogurt with the garlic and season with salt and pepper.

**4** Add the beetroot, reserving a little to garnish the top, and mix well. Garnish with mint leaves.

**Per portion** Energy 95kcal/403kJ; Protein 7.8g; Carbohydrate 14.4g, of which sugars 13g; Fat 1.4g, of which saturates 0.6g; Cholesterol 2mg; Calcium 249mg; Fibre 1.3g; Sodium 137mg.

# SALAD OF FETA, CHILLIES AND PARSLEY

*THERE ARE TWO COMMON SALADS EATEN AS MEZE, OR SERVED AS ACCOMPANIMENTS TO MEAT AND FISH DISHES. ONE, KNOWN AS ÇOBAN SALATASI, OR 'SHEPHERD'S SALAD', IS MADE OF CHOPPED CUCUMBER, TOMATOES, PEPPERS, ONION AND FLAT LEAF PARSLEY; THE OTHER IS THIS GYPSY SALAD, ÇINGENE PILAVI, MEANING 'GYPSY RICE'. THE MIX IS SIMILAR TO SHEPHERD'S SALAD, ONLY A CHILLI IS INCLUDED TO GIVE A FIERY KICK, AND CRUMBLED FETA IS ADDED TO REPRESENT THE RICE.*

SERVES THREE TO FOUR

INGREDIENTS

    2 red onions, cut in half lengthways
      and finely sliced along the grain
    1 green (bell) pepper, seeded
      and finely sliced
    1 fresh green chilli, seeded
      and chopped
    2–3 garlic cloves, chopped
    1 bunch of fresh flat leaf parsley,
      roughly chopped
    225g/8oz firm feta cheese,
      rinsed and grated
    2 large tomatoes, skinned,
      seeded and finely chopped
    30–45ml/2–3 tbsp olive oil
    salt and ground black pepper
To serve
    scant 5ml/1 tsp kırmızı biber,
      or paprika
    scant 5ml/1 tsp ground sumac

**1** Place the sliced red onions in a small bowl and sprinkle with a little salt. Leave for 10 minutes to draw out the onion juices, then transfer the onions to a sieve (strainer) and rinse under cold running water. Pat the onions dry with kitchen paper.

**VARIATION**
Omit the green chilli if you do not like spicy food.

**2** Mix the onions and green pepper in a bowl with the chilli, garlic, parsley, feta and tomatoes.

**3** Add the olive oil and salt and pepper to taste and toss well to combine everything thoroughly.

**4** Transfer the salad to a large serving dish and sprinkle with the kırmızı biber or paprika and sumac.

**Per portion** Energy 253kcal/1049kJ; Protein 11.1g; Carbohydrate 13.4g, of which sugars 11g; Fat 17.6g, of which saturates 8.6g; Cholesterol 39mg; Calcium 260mg; Fibre 3.2g; Sodium 824mg.

# MELON AND CHEESE SALAD WITH PASTIRMA

*ONE OF THE MOST TRADITIONAL MEZE DISHES IS A PLATE OF SWEET MELON CUT INTO CUBES, WHICH IS OFTEN COMBINED WITH CUBES OF WHITE CHEESE (BEYAZ PEYNIR) TO MAKE A VERY REFRESHING SNACK OR NIBBLE. A MODERN VERSION, CALLED KAVUN VE PEYNIR SALATASI, INCLUDES FINE STRIPS OF CURED BEEF, PASTIRMA, AND HERBS. DELICIOUS AS A FIRST COURSE, AN ACCOMPANIMENT TO GRILLED FOOD, OR AS PART OF A BUFFET SPREAD, THIS SIMPLE SALAD IS A DELIGHT TO THE SENSES.*

### SERVES FOUR TO SIX

INGREDIENTS

- 1 ripe juicy melon, such as Galia or honeydew
- 200g/7oz beyaz peynir, or plain feta cheese, cut into bitesize cubes
- 115g/4oz pastırma, very finely sliced with the coating (çemen) removed, and cut into thin strips
- 1 small bunch fresh green or purple basil leaves
- 30ml/2 tbsp olive oil
- juice of 1 lemon

**1** Cut the melon in half and scoop out the seeds with a spoon. Cut each half in half again and, using a sharp knife, remove the flesh from the skin and cut it into bitesize cubes.

**2** Put the melon and feta cubes into a shallow bowl, or in serving dish, and add the strips of pastırma and most of the basil leaves. Add the olive oil and lemon juice, and toss the salad gently.

**3** Garnish with the remaining basil and serve on its own, or with grilled (broiled) food or other meze dishes.

**COOK'S TIP**
Don't dress the salad too far in advance as the melon will emit a lot of juice and the basil leaves will wilt.

**Per portion** Energy 172kcal/716kJ; Protein 10.2g; Carbohydrate 5.4g, of which sugars 5.3g; Fat 12.4g, of which saturates 5.8g; Cholesterol 34mg; Calcium 145mg; Fibre 0.7g; Sodium 520mg.

# TOMATO, PEPPER AND CHILLI SALAD

*The Turkish word taze means fresh, which is exactly what this meze dish is — a mixture of chopped fresh vegetables. Along with cubes of melon and feta, or plump olives spiked with red pepper and oregano, this is meze at its simplest and best. Popular in kebab houses, taze ezmesi is good served with chunks of warm, crusty bread or toasted pitta.*

### SERVES FOUR

INGREDIENTS

2 large tomatoes, skinned, seeded and finely chopped
2 Turkish green peppers or
  1 green (bell) pepper, seeded and finely chopped
1 onion, finely chopped
1 green chilli, seeded and finely chopped
1 small bunch of fresh flat leaf parsley, finely chopped
a few fresh mint leaves, finely chopped
15–30ml/1–2 tbsp olive oil
salt and ground black pepper
pitta bread, toasted, to serve

**1** Put the finely chopped tomatoes, peppers, onion, green chilli, flat leaf parsley and mint in a medium bowl and mix well together.

**2** Bind the mixture with oil and season with salt and pepper.

**3** To toast the pitta bread, first split it in half using a sharp knife, then place on a hot griddle for 1–2 minutes, turn, and toast for a further 1 minute.

**4** Serve the salad at room temperature with the toasted pitta.

**VARIATION**
To turn this salad into a paste, add 15–30ml/1–2 tbsp tomato purée (paste) with a little extra chilli and 5–10ml/ 1–2 tsp sugar when you bind the chopped vegetables with the olive oil. The mixture will become a tangy paste to spread on fresh, crusty bread or toasted pitta, and it can also be used as a sauce for grilled, broiled or barbecued meats.

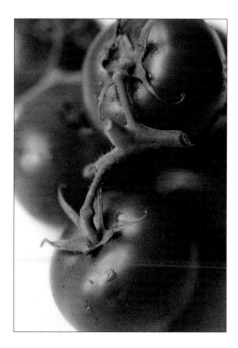

**Per portion** Energy 101kcal/420kJ; Protein 2.3g; Carbohydrate 9.3g, of which sugars 8g; Fat 6.3g, of which saturates 0.9g; Cholesterol 0mg; Calcium 66mg; Fibre 2.7g; Sodium 15mg.

# ORANGE AND ONION SALAD WITH OLIVES

*THIS REFRESHING SALAD, CALLED PORTAKAL SALATASI, IS POPULAR IN THE SOUTH OF TURKEY, NEAR THE SYRIAN BORDER, WHERE THE REGIONAL GÜNEY CUISINE IS PARTICULARLY FIERY. FROM MERSIN AND ADANA TO ANTAKYA AND GAZIANTEP, THERE ARE VARIATIONS OF THIS SALAD, SOME OF WHICH INCLUDE CHILLIES. SERVE WITH SPICY STEWS AND KEBABS*

SERVES FOUR

INGREDIENTS
    3 sweet, juicy oranges
    1 red onion, finely sliced in rings
    10–12 plump black olives,
      such as Kalamata
    5ml/1 tsp cumin seeds, crushed
    5ml/1 tsp ground sumac
    5ml/1 tsp dried thyme
    30–45ml/2–3 tbsp olive oil
    salt
    1 small bunch fresh mint leaves,
      torn or roughly chopped, to garnish

**VARIATIONS**
• Occasionally, finely sliced beetroot
(beet) is added to this salad, which lends
a pinkish-purple hue to the orange slices.
• Use pink grapefruit instead of orange.

**1** Place each orange on a board and, using a small, sharp knife, carefully cut away the peel and pith, making sure that no pith remains.

**2** Thinly slice the orange into rings and then either keep the rings whole or cut them into half-moon shapes. Do the same with the onion rings.

**3** Arrange the oranges and onions in a shallow bowl or a serving dish and add the olives. Sprinkle the cumin, sumac and thyme over the sliced oranges and onions and pour over the oil.

**4** Toss the salad gently, season with salt to taste, and sprinkle the mint leaves over the top to garnish.

**Per portion** Energy 150kcal/629kJ; Protein 3g; Carbohydrate 18.9g, of which sugars 16.4g; Fat 7.6g, of which saturates 1.1g; Cholesterol 0mg; Calcium 102mg; Fibre 3.8g; Sodium 292mg.

# BEAN SALAD

*SALADS MADE WITH HARICOT, SOYA, BORLOTTI OR BLACK-EYED BEANS ARE POPULAR AS MEZE DISHES, OR AS ACCOMPANIMENTS TO GRILLED, BROILED OR BARBECUED MEATS. OFTEN, THE SALADS ARE SIMPLY MADE FROM BEANS, ONIONS AND FLAT LEAF PARSLEY TOSSED IN OLIVE OIL. OTHERS, SUCH AS THIS, ARE MORE ELABORATE, AND MAKE A TASTY, HEALTHY, AND DELICIOUS LUNCH DISH.*

SERVES FOUR

INGREDIENTS

225g/8oz/1¼ cups dried haricot (navy), soya or black-eyed beans (peas), soaked in cold water for at least 6 hours or overnight
1 red onion, cut in half lengthways, in half again crossways, and sliced along the grain
45–60ml/3–4 tbsp black olives, drained
1 bunch of fresh flat leaf parsley, roughly chopped
60ml/4 tbsp olive oil
juice of 1 lemon
3–4 eggs, boiled until just firm, shelled and quartered
12 canned or bottled anchovy fillets, rinsed and drained
salt and ground black pepper
lemon wedges, to serve

**1** Drain the beans, transfer them to a pan and fill the pan with plenty of cold water. Bring the water to the boil and boil the beans for 1 minute, then lower the heat and partially cover the pan. Simmer for about 45 minutes, until the beans are cooked but still firm – they should have a bite to them, and not be soft and mushy.

**2** Drain the beans, rinse well under cold running water and remove any skins.

**3** Mix the beans in a wide, shallow bowl with the onion, olives and most of the parsley. Toss in the oil and lemon juice, and season with salt and pepper.

**4** Place the eggs and anchovy fillets on top of the salad and add the remaining parsley. Serve with lemon wedges.

**Per portion** Energy 402kcal/1674kJ; Protein 28g; Carbohydrate 10.4g, of which sugars 4.2g; Fat 28g, of which saturates 4.4g; Cholesterol 149mg; Calcium 221mg; Fibre 10g; Sodium 696mg.

# BULGUR SALAD

*COMBINING BULGUR WHEAT, VEGETABLES, MINT AND PARSLEY, KISIR IS SUSTAINING AND REFRESHING. IT TASTES FABULOUS SERVED AT ROOM TEMPERATURE AS PART OF A BUFFET OR BARBECUE SPREAD, WITH LEMON WEDGES FOR SQUEEZING OVER IT. IN SOME HOUSEHOLDS, IT IS OFFERED TO GUESTS BEFORE TEA IS SERVED, SPOONED ON TO VINE LEAVES AND ACCOMPANIED BY SLICES OF TOMATO AND SOME PICKLES.*

SERVES FOUR TO SIX

INGREDIENTS
    175g/6oz/1 cup bulgur wheat,
      rinsed and drained
    45–60ml/3–4 tbsp olive oil
    juice of 1–2 lemons
    30ml/2 tbsp tomato purée (paste)
    10ml/2 tsp sugar
    1 large or 2 small red onions,
      cut in half lengthways, in half
      again crossways, and sliced
      along the grain
    10ml/2 tsp kırmızı biber, or
      1–2 fresh red chillies, seeded
      and finely chopped
    1 bunch each of fresh mint
      and flat leaf parsley,
      finely chopped
    salt and ground black pepper
    a few fresh mint and parsley leaves,
      to garnish

**1** Put the bulgur wheat into a wide bowl, pour over enough boiling water to cover it by about 2.5cm/1in, and give it a quick stir. Cover the bowl with a plate or a pan lid and leave the bulgur wheat to steam for about 25 minutes, until it has soaked up the water and doubled in quantity.

**VARIATION**
In the south-east of Turkey, where the juice of sour pomegranates is often used instead of lemons and hot red pepper is added liberally to food, a fiery kısır is moulded into small balls and served in lettuce-leaf wrappings.

**2** Pour the olive oil and squeeze the lemon juice over the bulgur and toss to mix.

**3** Add the tomato purée and toss the mixture again until everything is combined and the bulgur is well coated.

**4** Add the sugar, onion, kırmızı biber or chillies, and the chopped fresh herbs. Season with salt and pepper and mix well to combine.

**5** Serve at room temperature, garnished with a little mint and parsley.

**Per portion** Energy 149kcal/620kJ; Protein 3g; Carbohydrate 21.6g, of which sugars 5.4g; Fat 6.1g, of which saturates 0.8g; Cholesterol 0mg; Calcium 54mg; Fibre 1.7g; Sodium 19mg.

# FRIED AUBERGINE, COURGETTE AND PEPPER WITH YOGURT AND POMEGRANATE

*THIS VERY SIMPLE, TASTY DISH, CALLED ŞAKŞUKA, SEEMS TO CAUSE A CERTAIN AMOUNT OF DEBATE IN TURKEY, AS IT VARIES HUGELY ACROSS THE COUNTRY. HOWEVER, THE ONE COMMON DENOMINATOR IS THAT ALL VERSIONS INCLUDE COOKED VEGETABLES SERVED WITH YOGURT. THIS COLOURFUL VERSION IS FROM THE MEDITERRANEAN REGION AND IS DELICIOUS SERVED ON ITS OWN WITH BREAD.*

SERVES FOUR

INGREDIENTS
  1 large aubergine (eggplant)
  1 courgette (zucchini)
  1 red (bell) pepper
  sunflower oil, for deep-frying
  4 Turkish çarliston peppers,
    kept whole with stalk
  200ml/7fl oz/scant 1 cup thick
    and creamy natural (plain) yogurt
  2–3 garlic cloves, crushed
  30–45ml/2–3 tbsp pomegranate
    seeds
  salt and ground black pepper

**1** Using a vegetable peeler, partially peel the aubergine in stripes.

**2** Cut the aubergine in half lengthways and then cut each half into thick slices. Drop the slices into a bowl of salted water to prevent them discolouring. Drain and squeeze them dry before frying, otherwise the excess water will cause the hot oil to spatter everywhere.

**3** Cut the courgette in half lengthways and then cut it widthways into thick slices. Deseed the pepper and cut it into bitesize pieces.

**4** Heat enough oil for deep-frying in a wide pan. Fry the vegetables in batches, until they are golden brown. Lift them out of the oil with tongs or a slotted spoon and drain on kitchen paper.

**5** In a bowl, beat the yogurt with the garlic, and season to taste with salt and pepper. Pile the hot vegetables on to a serving dish and spoon the yogurt over the top, reserving 15–30ml/1–2 tbsp in the base of the bowl.

**6** Fold half the pomegranate seeds into the remaining yogurt and spoon the mixture over the top of the prepared dish. Garnish with the remainder of the pomegranate seeds.

**7** Serve immediately, while the vegetables are still warm, to contrast with the cool yogurt. Accompany with chunks of fresh, crusty bread to scoop and mop up the tasty sauce.

**COOK'S TIPS**
• A fruit from antiquity, the pomegranate has symbolized beauty, fertility and prosperity and, according to the medieval Islamic mystics, it purged the soul of anger and envy. Cultivated in the Middle East, it has long been used in the cooking of this region, and is also thought by some to have magical properties. The ruby-red grains of sweet pomegranates are eaten fresh, whereas the sour fruits are used in soups, marinades, dressings and syrups, and to make a cooling sherbet drink.
• To extract the seeds from a pomegranate, cut the fruit into quarters and invert each quarter by pushing the skin with your thumbs. Some seeds will fall out; the rest you will have to pick out individually.

**Per portion** Energy 225kcal/933kJ; Protein 6.5g; Carbohydrate 13.3g, of which sugars 11.6g; Fat 17.1g, of which saturates 4.2g; Cholesterol 0mg; Calcium 104mg; Fibre 4g; Sodium 43mg.

# ROASTED COURGETTES AND PEACHES WITH PINE NUTS

*A FAVOURITE DISH IN TURKEY IS A MIXTURE OF DEEP-FRIED OR GRILLED VEGETABLES SERVED WITH A GARLIC-FLAVOURED SAUCE MADE WITH YOGURT, NUTS OR SESAME PASTE. COURGETTES, AUBERGINES AND CARROTS ARE THE MOST COMMON VEGETABLES USED, AND THEY ARE OFTEN DEEP-FRIED IN BATTER. THIS RECIPE, HOWEVER, COMBINES FRUIT AND VEGETABLES TO MAKE A COLOURFUL MEDLEY THAT IS BAKED RATHER THAN DEEP-FRIED OR GRILLED. YOU CAN SERVE IT ON ITS OWN WITH A YOGURT OR TARATOR SAUCE, OR A TAHINI DRESSING, AND WARM, CRUSTY BREAD, OR AS AN ACCOMPANIMENT TO GRILLED, BROILED OR BARBECUED MEAT OR POULTRY.*

## SERVES FOUR

### INGREDIENTS
2 courgettes (zucchini)
2 yellow or red (bell) peppers,
  seeded and cut into wedges
100ml/3½ fl oz/scant ½ cup
  olive oil
4–6 plum tomatoes
2 firm peaches, peeled, halved and
  stoned (pitted), then cut into wedges
30ml/2 tbsp pine nuts
salt and ground black pepper
For the yogurt sauce
500g/1¼ lb/2¼ cups thick and
  creamy natural (plain) yogurt
2–3 garlic cloves, crushed
juice of ½ lemon

### VARIATIONS
This dish is also delicious served with tarator sauce or tahini dressing.
• To make the tarator sauce, sprinkle 1–2 slices of day-old bread with a little water, leave for a few minutes until the water is absorbed, then squeeze dry. Roughly pound 115g/4oz/⅔ cup shelled walnuts, hazelnuts, almonds or pine nuts to a paste with 1–2 garlic cloves and the bread. Beat in the juice of ½ lemon and drizzle in enough olive oil to form a thick, creamy sauce, beating all the time as when making mayonnaise. Season with salt and ground black pepper.
• To make tahini dressing, thin down about 30ml/2 tbsp sesame paste with a little water and lemon juice, beat in some crushed garlic and, if you like, a little roasted kırmızı biber. Season with salt and ground black pepper. This can be used as a dressing for roasted or steamed vegetables or for a salad of carrots, red onion and chickpeas tossed with chopped fresh mint, parsley and coriander (cilantro).

**1** Preheat the oven to 200°C/400°F/ Gas 6. Using a vegetable peeler, peel the courgettes lengthways in stripes like a zebra, then halve and slice them lengthways, or cut into wedges.

**2** Place the courgettes and peppers in a baking dish, preferably an earthenware one. Drizzle the oil over them and sprinkle with salt, then bake in the oven for 20 minutes.

**3** Take the dish out of the oven and turn the vegetables in the oil, then mix in the tomatoes and peaches. Bake for a further 20–25 minutes, until everything is nicely browned.

**4** Meanwhile, make the yogurt sauce. In a small bowl, beat the yogurt with the garlic and lemon juice. Season to taste with salt and pepper and set aside until required, or chill in the refrigerator.

**5** Dry-roast the pine nuts in a small, heavy pan, shaking them constantly, until they turn golden brown and give off a nutty aroma. Be careful not to let them burn. Remove from the heat.

**6** When the roasted vegetables are ready, remove the dish from the oven and sprinkle the pine nuts over the top. Serve immediately with the yogurt sauce and some warm bread.

**Per portion** Energy 362kcal/1507kJ; Protein 11.7g; Carbohydrate 26.7g, of which sugars 26.3g; Fat 24.1g, of which saturates 3.7g; Cholesterol 2mg; Calcium 284mg; Fibre 4.8g; Sodium 120mg.

# WARM AUBERGINE SALAD

*IN TURKEY, AUBERGINES ARE OFTEN GRILLED OR BAKED TO BE USED IN A VARIETY OF MEZE DISHES, INCLUDING THIS SALAD. ALTHOUGH PATLICAN SALATASI CAN VARY, THE RESULT IS ALWAYS FRESH-TASTING. IT IS BEST SERVED WHILE THE FLESH IS STILL WARM, BUT IT CAN ALSO BE MADE IN ADVANCE AND SERVED AT ROOM TEMPERATURE. SERVE ON ITS OWN WITH BREAD OR AS PART OF A MEZE SPREAD.*

**2** Smoke the aubergines and the red pepper directly over the gas flame, over hot charcoal or under the grill (broiler).

**3** When the skin of the pepper has buckled and browned, plunge it immediately under cold running water and peel off the skin. Remove the stalk and seeds, chop the softened flesh, and set aside.

**4** When the aubergines are soft, place them on a board and slit them open. Scoop out the warm flesh, taking care to leave the skin behind (this is easier if the aubergines have been grilled over charcoal as the skin toughens up).

**5** Place the flesh in a wide bowl (some cooks like to chop it; others keep it in clumps). Add the pepper, spring onions, tomatoes, hot green pepper, parsley and dill.

**6** Add the olive oil, lemon juice and garlic, and toss well to combine thoroughly. Season to taste, and serve while still deliciously warm, with fresh crusty bread to scoop it up.

SERVES FOUR TO SIX

INGREDIENTS
  2 tomatoes
  2 large aubergines (eggplants),
    or 4 small thin ones
  1 red (bell) pepper
  4–6 spring onions (scallions),
    trimmed and finely chopped
  2 hot green peppers, or 1 green
    chilli, seeded and finely sliced
  1 good-sized bunch flat leaf parsley,
    leaves chopped
  1 small bunch dill fronds, chopped
  45–60ml/3–4 tbsp olive oil
  juice of 1–2 lemons
  2–4 garlic cloves, crushed
  salt and ground black pepper

**1** Plunge the tomatoes into boiling water for 30 seconds, then refresh in cold water. Peel away the skins. Remove the seeds and chop the flesh.

**Per portion** Energy 102kcal/424kJ; Protein 3.2g; Carbohydrate 8.2g, of which sugars 7.5g; Fat 6.5g, of which saturates 1g; Cholesterol 0mg; Calcium 59mg; Fibre 4g; Sodium 14mg.

# JEWELLED MACKEREL SALAD <u>IN A</u> DOME

*THIS SALAD, USKUMRU SALATASI, CAN BE SERVED AS A MEZE DISH OR AS A LIGHT MEAL. GENERALLY, IT IS MADE WITH FRESH MACKEREL, BUT SOME COOKS LIKE TO MAKE IT WITH THE SMOKED FISH, WHICH MAKES THE OVERALL DISH HEAVIER. THE TURKS PRESENT THIS DISH ATTRACTIVELY, MAKING IT AN IDEAL SALAD FOR A BUFFET SPREAD, OR AN IMPRESSIVE FIRST COURSE AT A DINNER PARTY.*

SERVES TWO TO FOUR

INGREDIENTS
15ml/1 tbsp currants
3 tomatoes
sunflower oil, for shallow-frying
2 fresh mackerel, gutted and
  thoroughly cleaned
45ml/3 tbsp pine nuts
30ml/2 tbsp olive oil
1 crisp cos or romaine lettuce,
  cut into thin strips
a handful of fresh rocket
  (arugula) leaves
1 bunch fresh dill fronds,
  stalks removed
1 red onion, sliced into thin rings
For the dressing
60–75ml/4–5 tbsp olive oil
juice of 1 lemon
15ml/1 tbsp apple or white
  wine vinegar
5ml/1 tsp yellow mustard
5–10ml/1–2 tsp clear honey
salt and ground black pepper

**1** Soak the currants in warm water for 15 minutes then drain them.

**2** Plunge the tomatoes into a large bowl of boiling water for 30 seconds, then refresh immediately in cold water. Peel away the tomato skins with your fingers, then remove the seeds and cut the flesh into thin strips (reserve one round slice for the top of the dome).

**3** Heat enough sunflower oil in a heavy pan for shallow-frying the mackerel.

**4** Fry the mackerel for 5–6 minutes on each side. Drain on kitchen paper and leave to cool. Alternatively, you can grill (broil) the mackerel.

**5** Peel the skin off the mackerel and cut the flesh into long fingers.

**6** In a small, heavy pan, fry the pine nuts in the olive oil, until they begin to colour. Toss in the currants to plump them up, then pour them on to kitchen paper to drain. Leave to cool.

**7** Arrange the lettuce and rocket leaves in a dome in the centre of a round serving dish. Arrange the mackerel fingers around the sides of the dome, laying them gently on top of the leaves, and interspersing them with strips of tomato. Place the reserved slice of tomato on the very top of the dome.

**8** Decorate the dome with the dill fronds, placing a little sprig in the centre of the sliced tomato, and arrange the onion rings around the base.

**9** Sprinkle the pine nuts and currants over the dome and around the base. The whole effect should be like an elaborately jewelled crown.

**10** To make the dressing, mix together all the dressing ingredients in a bowl and season to taste. Pour the dressing over the salad and serve immediately, with fresh, crusty bread.

**Per portion** Energy 575kcal/2383kJ; Protein 27.2g; Carbohydrate 9.5g, of which sugars 9.5g; Fat 47.8g, of which saturates 7.6g; Cholesterol 66mg; Calcium 60mg; Fibre 2.2g; Sodium 121mg.

# Soups and Hot Meze

In every village, town and city, soup stalls and soup houses do brisk business, serving at all hours of the day. In rural Anatolia dishes such as Meadow Yogurt Soup with Rice and Mint are often eaten for breakfast, whereas in Istanbul late-night revellers head to the nearest işkembici, to tuck into Classic Tripe Soup. When not snacking on one of their favourite soups, Turks may well be eating a hot snack, such as Chickpea Parcels or Filo Cigars Filled with Feta, Parsley, Mint and Dill.

# POMEGRANATE BROTH

*WITH ITS ORIGINS IN PERSIA AND AZERBAIJAN, THIS FRESH-TASTING, DELICATE BROTH, NARLI ÇORBA, IS PERHAPS THE BEST WAY OF APPRECIATING THE COLOUR AND FLAVOUR OF SOUR POMEGRANATES, AS IT IS PLEASING TO BOTH THE EYE AND THE TASTE BUDS. CLEAR AND REFRESHING, IT IS USUALLY SERVED AS A SOPHISTICATED PALATE CLEANSER BETWEEN COURSES, OR AS A LIGHT APPETIZER AT THE START OF A MEAL. SOUR POMEGRANATES ARE OFTEN AVAILABLE IN MIDDLE EASTERN STORES, BUT IF YOU CAN ONLY FIND SWEET POMEGRANATES, USE THEM IN THE SAME WAY, BUT STIR IN THE JUICE OF ONE LEMON TO ADD THE DESIRED ACIDITY AND TARTNESS.*

SERVES FOUR

INGREDIENTS
    5–6 sour or sweet pomegrantes
    1.2 litres/2 pints/5 cups clear
      chicken stock
    juice of 1 lemon, if using
      sweet pomegranates
    seeds of 1 sweet pomegranate
    salt and ground black pepper
    fresh mint leaves, to garnish

**COOK'S TIP**
Do not use any metal other than stainless steel for squeezing or it will cause the juice to discolour and taste unpleasant.

**1** For 150ml/¼ pint/⅔ cup juice, you will need 5–6 sour pomegranates. Cut the pomegranates in half and extract the juice with a stainless-steel, glass or wooden lemon squeezer.

**2** Pour the stock into a pan and bring to the boil. Lower the heat, stir in the pomegranate juice, and lemon juice if using sweet pomegranates, then bring the stock back to the boil.

**3** Lower the heat again and stir in half the pomegranate seeds, then season and turn off the heat.

**4** Ladle into wamed bowls. Sprinkle the remaining pomegranate seeds over the top and garnish with mint leaves.

**Per portion** Energy 62kcal/260kJ; Protein 2g; Carbohydrate 3.9g, of which sugars 2.3g; Fat 4.4g, of which saturates 0.4g; Cholesterol 0mg; Calcium 14mg; Fibre 0.6g; Sodium 205mg.

# FISH BROTH <u>WITH</u> CELERIAC

*WITH SUCH AN EXTENSIVE COASTLINE, THERE IS A WIDE CHOICE OF FISH AVAILABLE IN TURKEY FOR MAKING THIS CLASSIC FISH SOUP — BALIK ÇORBASI — RANGING FROM SEA BASS, BLUE FISH, SCORPION FISH, MACKEREL, BONITO, TURBOT AND RED MULLET. ALONG THE BLACK SEA, THE LOCAL SOUP INVARIABLY INCLUDES SOME SALTY ANCHOVIES; IN CENTRAL ANATOLIA THE FRESHWATER FISH, SUCH AS CARP, ARE OCCASIONALLY USED IN THE SOUP, ALTHOUGH IN PARTS OF EASTERN ANATOLIA FISH SOUP IS UNHEARD OF. HOWEVER, WHATEVER THE VARIETY OF FISH AVAILABLE FOR USE, THE METHOD OF MAKING THE SOUP VARIES LITTLE FROM REGION TO REGION.*

SERVES FOUR TO SIX

INGREDIENTS

500g/1¼lb fresh fish, such as trout, cod or sea bass
250g/9oz prawns (shrimp)
2 onions, quartered with their skins on
4–6 peppercorns
1 whole celeriac
2 potatoes, peeled and diced
2 carrots, peeled and diced
1 small bunch celery leaves, coarsely chopped
1 small bunch flat leaf parsley, leaves coarsely chopped
2 garlic cloves, crushed
15ml/1 tbsp vinegar
salt and ground black pepper
1 lemon, cut into wedges, to serve

**1** First prepare the stock. Skin and fillet the fish and shell the prawns. Cut the fillets into bitesize pieces and set them aside with the prawns.

**2** Put the fish head and bones with the prawn shells into a large, heavy pan. Add the onions and peppercorns and about 2.5 litres/4 pints/10¼ cups water.

**3** Bring the water to the boil, reduce the heat and simmer for 25–30 minutes, skimming the top to remove any scum. Strain the stock into another pan.

**4** Peel and dice the celeriac, and cover with water until ready to use. Bring the stock to the boil and stir in the diced vegetables. Reduce the heat and simmer for about 15 minutes, or until the vegetables are tender.

**5** Stir in the celery leaves and parsley, and add the fish fillets and prawns. Simmer for about 5 minutes or until the fish and prawns are cooked.

**6** Season with salt and pepper to taste, and stir in the garlic and vinegar to sharpen the flavours.

**7** Ladle the broth into heated serving bowls and serve with wedges of lemon to squeeze into it to give both sweet and sour notes in every mouthful.

**Per portion** Energy 169kcal/712kJ; Protein 24.9g; Carbohydrate 14.9g, of which sugars 7.1g; Fat 1.5g, of which saturates 0.2g; Cholesterol 120mg; Calcium 117mg; Fibre 3.3g; Sodium 195mg.

# MEADOW YOGURT SOUP WITH RICE AND MINT

*IN EVERY SOUP HOUSE, BUS STATION AND ROADSIDE CAFÉ THROUGHOUT TURKEY, YOU WILL COME ACROSS YOGURT SOUP. BASED ON WELL-FLAVOURED STOCK AND YOGURT, IT USUALLY CONTAINS A LITTLE RICE, BULGUR, CHICKPEAS OR BARLEY, DEPENDING ON WHICH REGION YOU ARE IN, AND OCCASIONALLY IT IS COLOURED WITH SAFFRON OR SPRINKLED WITH PAPRIKA. WHEN IT IS FLAVOURED WITH DRIED MINT, IT IS CALLED YAYLA ÇORBASI, OR MEADOW SOUP.*

**3** Stir in the rice and most of the mint, reserving a little for the garnish. Lower the heat, cover the pan and simmer for about 20 minutes, until the rice is cooked. Season with salt and pepper.

**4** Beat the yogurt until smooth, then spoon almost all of it into the soup. Keep the heat low and stir vigorously to make sure the yogurt remains smooth and creamy and becomes well blended.

**5** Ladle the soup into serving bowls, swirl in the remaining yogurt, and garnish with the remaining mint.

SERVES FOUR

INGREDIENTS
  15ml/1 tbsp butter or sunflower oil
  1 large onion, finely chopped
  scant 15ml/1 tbsp plain
    (all-purpose) flour
  1.2 litres/2 pints/5 cups lamb or
    chicken stock
  75g/3oz/scant ½ cup long grain rice
    (wild or plain), well rinsed
  15–30ml/1–2 tbsp dried mint
  400ml/14fl oz/1⅔ cups thick and
    creamy natural (plain) yogurt,
    strained (*see* Cook's Tip)
  salt and ground black pepper

**1** Melt the butter or oil in a heavy pan, add the onion and cook until soft.

**2** Take the pan off the heat and stir in the flour, then pour in the stock, stirring constantly. Return to the heat and bring the stock to the boil, stirring often.

**COOK'S TIP**
If you can't get strained yogurt you can make it yourself. Line a sieve (strainer) with a piece of muslin (cheesecloth) and spoon thick and creamy natural (plain) yogurt into it. Allow the excess liquid to drip through the muslin, then transfer the yogurt from the sieve to a bowl.

**Per portion** Energy 187kcal/781kJ; Protein 7.6g; Carbohydrate 30.3g, of which sugars 11.1g; Fat 4.4g, of which saturates 2.5g; Cholesterol 9mg; Calcium 215mg; Fibre 1g; Sodium 108mg.

# LEEK SOUP WITH FETA, DILL AND PAPRIKA

*CREAMY LEEK SOUP IS A POPULAR HOME-COOKED DISH IN TURKEY. FLAVOURED WITH DILL AND TOPPED WITH CRUMBLED WHITE CHEESE, THIS ONE IS WARMING AND SATISFYING. THE SALTINESS OF FETA IS GOOD IN THIS SOUP, BUT YOU COULD JUST AS WELL USE ROQUEFORT OR PARMESAN, BOTH OF WHICH ARE EQUALLY SALTY, AND YOU COULD SUBSTITUTE CROÛTONS FOR THE CHEESE. SERVE WITH CHUNKS OF FRESH, CRUSTY BREAD AS AN APPETIZER, OR AS A LIGHT MEAL ON ITS OWN.*

## SERVES THREE TO FOUR

### INGREDIENTS

- 30ml/2 tbsp olive or sunflower oil
- 3 leeks, trimmed, roughly chopped and washed
- 1 onion, chopped
- 5ml/1 tsp sugar
- 1 bunch of fresh dill, chopped, with a few fronds reserved for the garnish
- 300ml/½ pint/1¼ cups milk
- 15ml/1 tbsp butter (optional)
- 115g/4oz feta cheese, crumbled
- salt and ground black pepper
- paprika, to garnish

**5** Ladle the soup into bowls and top with the crumbled feta. Serve immediately, garnished with a little paprika and the dill fronds.

**1** Heat the oil in a heavy pan and stir in the chopped leeks and onion. Cook for about 10 minutes, or until the vegetables are soft.

**2** Add the sugar and chopped dill, and pour in 600ml/1 pint/2½ cups water. Bring to the boil, lower the heat and simmer for about 15 minutes. Leave the liquid to cool a little, then process in a blender until smooth.

**3** Return the puréed soup to the pan, pour in the milk and stir over a gentle heat until it is hot (don't let it come to the boil).

**4** Season with a little salt and plenty of freshly ground black pepper, bearing in mind that the feta is salty. If using the butter, drop it on to the surface of the soup and let it melt.

**Per portion** Energy 203kcal/844kJ; Protein 10g; Carbohydrate 10.9g, of which sugars 9.4g; Fat 13.5g, of which saturates 5.7g; Cholesterol 25mg; Calcium 259mg; Fibre 4.1g; Sodium 454mg.

# PUMPKIN SOUP WITH YOGURT

*THIS SIMPLE PURÉED SOUP — BAL KABAĞI ÇORBASI — IS A GREAT WINTER TREAT. PUMPKIN SELLERS SET UP THEIR STALLS IN THE STREETS AND DEFTLY PEEL AND SEED HUGE WEDGES OF PUMPKIN FOR PASSERS-BY, SO ALL THEY HAVE TO DO IS GO HOME AND POACH IT IN SYRUP FOR THE SWEET-SCENTED DESSERT, BAL KABAĞI TATLISI, OR TRANSFORM IT INTO THIS NOURISHING SOUP OF SWEET PUMPKIN FLESH AND TART, CREAMY YOGURT. TRADITIONALLY, MELTED BUTTER IS DRIZZLED OVER THE TOP.*

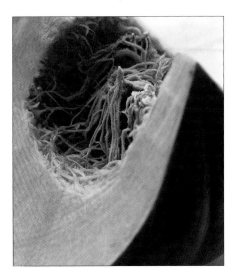

### SERVES THREE TO FOUR

INGREDIENTS
 1kg/2¼lb prepared pumpkin flesh,
  cut into cubes
 1 litre/1¾ pints/4 cups
  chicken stock
 10ml/2 tsp sugar
 25g/1oz/2 tbsp butter, or ghee
 60–75ml/4–5 tbsp thick and
  creamy natural (plain) yogurt
 salt and ground black pepper

**COOK'S TIP**
If pumpkins are not in season, you can use butternut squash instead.

**1** Put the pumpkin cubes into a pan with the stock, and bring the liquid to the boil. Reduce the heat, cover the pan, and simmer for about 20 minutes, or until the pumpkin is tender.

**2** Liquidize (blend) the soup in a blender, or use a potato masher to mash the flesh. Return the soup to the pan and bring it to the boil again.

**3** Add the sugar to the pan and season to taste with salt and pepper. Keep the pan over a low heat while you gently melt the butter or ghee in a small pan over a low heat.

**4** Pour the soup into a tureen, or ladle it into individual serving bowls. Swirl a little yogurt on to the surface of the soup and drizzle the melted butter over the top.

**5** Serve immediately, offering extra yogurt so that you can enjoy the contrasting burst of sweet and tart in each mouthful.

**Per portion** Energy 97kcal/406kJ; Protein 2.6g; Carbohydrate 9.3g, of which sugars 8g; Fat 5.8g, of which saturates 3.6g; Cholesterol 14mg; Calcium 104mg; Fibre 2.5g; Sodium 51mg.

# SPICY RED LENTIL SOUP WITH ONION

*IN ISTANBUL AND IZMIR, LENTIL SOUPS ARE LIGHT AND SUBTLY SPICED, AND SERVED AS AN APPETIZER OR AS A SNACK. IN ANATOLIA, LENTIL AND BEAN SOUPS ARE MADE WITH CHUNKS OF MUTTON AND FLAVOURED WITH TOMATO AND SPICES, AND ARE USUALLY SERVED AS A MEAL ON THEIR OWN. THIS RECIPE IS FOR A MEATLESS SOUP IN WHICH THE GARNISHINGS PLAY AN IMPORTANT ROLE. OFTEN, THE ONION, PARSLEY AND LEMON WILL BE PLACED IN A SEPARATE BOWL SO YOU CAN HELP YOURSELF.*

SERVES FOUR

INGREDIENTS
- 30–45ml/2–3 tbsp olive or vegetable oil
- 1 large onion, finely chopped
- 2 garlic cloves, finely chopped
- 1 fresh red chilli, seeded and chopped
- 5–10ml/1–2 tsp cumin seeds
- 5–10ml/1–2 tsp coriander seeds
- 1 carrot, finely chopped
- scant 5ml/1 tsp ground fenugreek
- 5ml/1 tsp sugar
- 15ml/1 tbsp tomato purée (paste)
- 250g/9oz/generous 1 cup split red lentils
- 1.75 litres/3 pints/7½ cups chicken stock
- salt and ground black pepper

To serve
- 1 small red onion, finely chopped
- 1 large bunch of fresh flat leaf parsley, finely chopped
- 4–6 lemon wedges

**1** Heat the oil in a heavy pan and stir in the onion, garlic, chilli, cumin and coriander seeds.

**2** When the onion begins to colour slightly, toss in the carrot and cook for 2–3 minutes.

**3** Add the fenugreek, sugar and tomato purée and stir in the lentils.

**4** Pour in the stock, stir well and bring to the boil. Lower the heat, partially cover the pan with a lid and simmer for 30–40 minutes, until the lentils have broken up.

**5** If the soup is too thick for your preference, thin it down to the desired consistency with a little water. Season with salt and pepper to taste.

**6** Serve the soup as it is or, if you prefer a smooth texture, leave it to cool slightly, then whiz it in a blender and reheat if necessary.

**7** Ladle the soup into bowls and sprinkle liberally with the chopped onion and parsley. Serve with a wedge of lemon to squeeze over the soup.

**Per portion** Energy 203kcal/856kJ; Protein 11.1g; Carbohydrate 31.8g, of which sugars 7.3g; Fat 4.4g, of which saturates 0.6g; Cholesterol 0mg; Calcium 45mg; Fibre 3.5g; Sodium 26mg.

# LAMB AND YOGURT SOUP

*DÜĞÜN ÇORBASI IS THE SOUP OF TURKISH WEDDINGS. STEEPED IN TRADITION, IT VARIES LITTLE THROUGHOUT THE COUNTRY, THE ONLY DIFFERENCE BEING THE INCLUSION OF CINNAMON TO FLAVOUR THE STOCK. MADE WITH LAMB STOCK AND CONTAINING CHUNKS OF COOKED LAMB, IT IS SLIGHTLY SOUR FROM THE CLASSIC LIAISON OF LEMON, EGG AND YOGURT.*

SERVES FOUR TO SIX

INGREDIENTS

500g/1¼lb lamb on the bone
  – neck, leg or shoulder
2 carrots, roughly chopped
2 potatoes, roughly chopped
1 cinnamon stick
45ml/3 tbsp thick and creamy
  (natural) plain yogurt
45ml/3 tbsp plain (all-purpose) flour
1 egg yolk
juice of ½ lemon
30ml/2 tbsp butter
5ml/1 tsp kırmızı biber, or paprika
salt and ground black pepper

**1** Place the lamb in a deep pan with the carrots, potatoes and cinnamon.

**2** Pour in 2 litres/3½ pints/8 cups water and bring to the boil over a high heat, then skim any scum off the surface and lower the heat.

**3** Cover the pan and simmer the mixture gently for about 1½ hours, or until the meat is so tender that it almost falls off the bone.

**4** Lift the lamb out of the pan using a slotted spoon, drain, and place it on a chopping board.

**5** Remove the meat from the bone and chop it into small pieces.

**6** Strain the stock and discard the carrots and potatoes. Pour the stock back into the pan, season and bring to the boil.

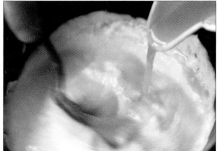

**7** In a deep bowl, beat the yogurt with the flour. Add the egg yolk and lemon juice and beat well again, then pour in about 250ml/8fl oz/1 cup of the hot stock, beating all the time so that the hot liquid doesn't cook the yolk.

**8** Lower the heat under the pan and pour the yogurt mixture into the stock, beating constantly.

**9** Add the meat to the pan and warm gently, ensuring the meat heats through but the mixture doesn't boil.

**10** Melt the butter in a small pan and stir in the kırmızı biber or paprika.

**11** Ladle the soup into bowls and drizzle the pepper butter over the top.

Per portion Energy 226kcal/943kJ; Protein 15g; Carbohydrate 14.4g, of which sugars 3.6g; Fat 12.4g, of which saturates 6.2g; Cholesterol 88mg; Calcium 54mg; Fibre 1.4g; Sodium 87mg.

# CLASSIC TRIPE SOUP

*REGARDED AS A FAITHFUL PICK-ME-UP, TERBIYELI İŞKEMBE ÇORBASI IS SOUGHT AFTER AT A REPUTED İŞKEMBECI (A CAFÉ THAT SPECIALISES IN TRIPE DISHES) LATE AT NIGHT. IT IS ALSO ONE OF THE CLASSIC DISHES PREPARED FOR THE RELIGIOUS FEAST, KURBAN BAYRAMI, WHEN EVERY PART OF THE SACRIFICED SHEEP IS USED TO MARK THE NEAR SACRIFICE OF ISAAC.*

SERVES FOUR TO SIX

INGREDIENTS
    225g/8oz lamb tripe, washed
    1.2 litres/2 pints/5 cups water
    15ml/1 tbsp butter or ghee
    25ml/1½ tbsp plain (all-purpose) flour
    1 egg yolk
    15ml/1 tbsp lemon juice
    salt and ground black pepper
To serve
    90ml/6 tbsp white wine vinegar
    1–3 garlic cloves, crushed
    25g/1oz/2 tbsp butter
    5ml/1 tsp kırmızı biber, or paprika

**1** Put the tripe into a large, heavy pan and cover with the water. Bring it to the boil and skim off any froth. Continue to boil for 20–25 minutes, until the tripe is tender. Drain and reserve the cooking liquid. Cut the tripe into fine strips.

**2** Melt the butter or ghee in a heavy pan and stir in the flour to make a roux. Pour in the cooking liquid, stirring until it thickens. Stir in the tripe, increase the heat, and simmer for 15–20 minutes.

**3** In a small bowl, beat the egg yolk with the lemon juice. Beat in two spoonfuls of the hot soup, then pour it back into the pan, stirring constantly to ensure the egg doesn't curdle. Season the soup with salt and pepper to taste.

**4** Pour the vinegar into a small bowl and beat in the crushed garlic to taste and a little salt.

**5** In a small pan, gently melt the butter and stir in the kırmızı biber or paprika.

**6** Ladle the soup into individual serving bowls and pour a little of the melted butter mixture over each one.

**7** Serve the soup immediately, passing around the spiked vinegar to drizzle over the top.

**Per portion** Energy 101kcal/421kJ; Protein 4.8g; Carbohydrate 4g, of which sugars 0.2g; Fat 7.5g, of which saturates 4.2g; Cholesterol 83mg; Calcium 41mg; Fibre 0.2g; Sodium 60mg.

# BAKED CHICKPEA PURÉE WITH LEMON AND PINE NUTS

*THIS RECIPE FOR BAKED HUMUS IS AN EASTERN ANATOLIAN SPECIALITY, AND MAKES A WELCOME CHANGE FROM THE STANDARD, COLD HUMUS THAT IS FOUND THROUGHOUT THE MIDDLE EAST. THICK AND GARLIC-FLAVOURED, IT VARIES SLIGHTLY IN TASTE, DEPENDING ON WHETHER YOU CHOOSE TO ADD SESAME PASTE AND CUMIN TO IT. ADDING YOGURT WILL MAKE IT LIGHTER IN TEXTURE. SERVE IT HOT AS PART OF A MEZE SPREAD OR AS A COMFORTING, SUSTAINING SNACK WITH GENEROUS HUNKS OF WARM, CRUSTY BREAD, TOASTED PITTA BREAD OR CHUNKS OF TURKISH PIDE. IT IS ALSO DELICIOUS SERVED AS A LIGHT LUNCH WITH A TOMATO AND HERB SALAD.*

SERVES FOUR

INGREDIENTS
    225g/8oz/1¼ cups dried chickpeas,
        soaked in cold water for at least
        6 hours or overnight
    about 50ml/2fl oz/¼ cup olive oil
    juice of 2 lemons
    3–4 garlic cloves, crushed
    10ml/2 tsp cumin seeds, crushed
    30–45ml/2–3 tbsp light sesame
        paste (tahini)
    45–60ml/3–4 heaped tbsp thick
        and creamy natural (plain) yogurt
    30–45ml/2–3 tbsp pine nuts
    40g/1½oz/3 tbsp butter or ghee
    5–10ml/1–2 tsp oiled or roasted
        Turkish red pepper or paprika
    salt and ground black pepper

**1** Drain the chickpeas, transfer them to a pan and fill the pan with plenty of cold water. Bring to the boil and boil for 1 minute, then lower the heat and partially cover the pan.

**2** Simmer the chickpeas for 1 hour, until they are soft and easy to mash.

**3** Drain the chickpeas, then rinse them well under cold running water. Remove any loose skins by rubbing the chickpeas in a clean kitchen towel. Preheat the oven to 200°C/400°F/Gas 6.

**4** Using a large mortar and pestle, pound the chickpeas with the oil, lemon juice, garlic and cumin.

**5** Beat in the sesame paste, then beat in the yogurt until the purée is light and smooth. Season to taste.

**6** Transfer the purée to an ovenproof dish – preferably an earthenware one – and smooth the top with the back of a spoon.

**7** Dry-roast the pine nuts in a small, heavy pan over a medium heat until golden brown. Lower the heat, add the butter and let it melt, then stir in the red pepper or paprika.

**8** Pour the mixture over the humus and bake for about 25 minutes, until it has risen slightly and the butter has been absorbed. Serve straight from the oven.

**Per portion** Energy 433kcal/1803kJ; Protein 15g; Carbohydrate 29.5g, of which sugars 3g; Fat 29.2g, of which saturates 7.7g; Cholesterol 21mg; Calcium 160mg; Fibre 6.8g; Sodium 91mg.

# COURGETTE AND APPLE WITH A HAZELNUT AND LEMON SAUCE

*STEAMED, FRIED, GRILLED OR ROASTED VEGETABLES ARE OFTEN SERVED WITH A NUT SAUCE, TARATOR, IN TURKEY. IN THIS RECIPE — TARATORLU KABAK — THE COURGETTES AND APPLES ARE ROASTED, BUT THEY COULD BE COOKED BY ANY METHOD, SUCH AS GRILLING OR STEAMING. ALONG THE BLACK SEA COAST, THE NUT SAUCE IS OFTEN MADE WITH THE LOCAL HAZELNUTS, WHICH MAKES A LIGHTER SAUCE THAN A WALNUT VERSION AND IS NOT AS CREAMY AS ONE MADE WITH PINE NUTS OR ALMONDS. THIS DISH CAN BE SERVED AS A SIDE DISH TO GRILLED AND ROASTED MEATS, OR AS A HOT MEZE DISH.*

SERVES FOUR

INGREDIENTS
  2 firm, fat courgettes (zucchini)
  2 sweet, firm red, pink, or
    yellow apples
  30–45ml/2–3 tbsp olive oil
  15–30ml/1–2 tbsp chopped
    roasted hazelnuts, to garnish
For the nut sauce
  115g/4oz/²/₃ cup hazelnuts
  1–2 garlic cloves
  30ml/2 tbsp olive oil
  juice of 1 lemon
  15ml/1 tbsp grape pekmez, or
    molasses or clear honey
  salt and ground black pepper

**1** Preheat the oven to 180°C/350°F/ Gas 4. Using a vegetable peeler, partially peel the courgettes in stripes. Slice them on the diagonal. Quarter and core the apples then cut each quarter into 2 or 3 segments.

**2** Place the courgette and apple slices in an ovenproof dish and pour over the olive oil. Put into the oven and roast for 35–40 minutes, or until golden brown.

**COOK'S TIP**
Other vegetables served this way include whole Mediterranean (bell) peppers, sliced aubergine (eggplant), pumpkin and squash, and fruit, such as plums.

**3** Meanwhile, make the nut sauce. Using a mortar and pestle, or a food processor, pound the hazelnuts with the garlic to form a thick paste.

**4** Gradually beat in the oil and lemon juice, until the mixture is quite creamy. Sweeten with the pekmez, molasses or clear honey, and season to taste.

**5** Arrange the roasted courgette and apple on a serving dish and drizzle the nut sauce over them. Sprinkle the roasted hazelnuts over the top and serve while still warm.

Per portion Energy 365kcal/1513kJ; Protein 6.6g; Carbohydrate 13.3g, of which sugars 12.6g; Fat 32.1g, of which saturates 3.2g; Cholesterol 0mg; Calcium 74mg; Fibre 4.2g; Sodium 5mg.

# TOMATO AND PEPPER RAGOÛT WITH EGGS

*MENEMEN IS TURKISH STREET FOOD. COOKED ON MAKESHIFT STOVES AT BUS AND TRAIN STATIONS, PORTS AND REST HOUSES, IT IS A SATISFYING SNACK OR MEAL. DEPENDING ON THE COOK, THE EGGS ARE EITHER STIRRED INTO THE RAGOÛT TO SCRAMBLE THEM, OR THEY ARE CRACKED ON TOP AND COOKED IN THE STEAM OF A DOMED LID UNTIL JUST SET.*

**4** Crack the eggs over the top of the tomato mixture, cover the pan and cook until the eggs are just done.

**5** Meanwhile, beat the yogurt with the garlic in a bowl and season with salt and pepper.

**6** Ladle the soup into bowls and serve hot, topped with parsley and dollops of garlic-flavoured yogurt.

**COOK'S TIPS**
• If you like, you can divide the tomato mixture between four small pans and crack an egg into each one, so that each person has their own serving.
• For breakfast, you will often be served the scrambled version of this dish that generally omits the (bell) pepper. It is fabulous served on toasted bread.

### SERVES FOUR

INGREDIENTS
   15ml/1 tbsp olive oil
   15ml/1 tbsp butter
   2 red onions, cut in half lengthways
      and sliced along the grain
   1 red or green (bell) pepper, halved
      lengthways, seeded and sliced
   2 garlic cloves, roughly chopped
   5–10ml/1–2 tsp kırmızı biber,
      or 1 fresh red chilli, seeded
      and sliced
   400g/14oz can chopped tomatoes
   5–10ml/1–2 tsp sugar
   4 eggs
   salt and ground black pepper
To serve
   90ml/6 tbsp thick and creamy
      natural (plain) yogurt
   1–2 garlic cloves, crushed
   a handful of fresh flat leaf parsley,
      roughly chopped

**1** Heat the oil and butter in a frying pan. Stir in the onions, pepper, garlic and kırmızı biber or chilli and cook until they begin to soften but not brown.

**2** Add the tomatoes and sugar to the pan and mix them in well.

**3** Cook for about 10 minutes, or until the liquid has reduced and the mixture is quite thick, then season with salt and pepper to taste.

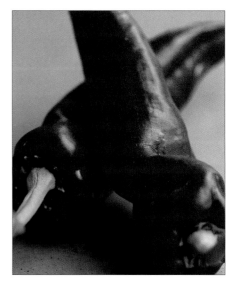

**Per portion** Energy 190kcal/790kJ; Protein 8.6g; Carbohydrate 14.9g, of which sugars 12.4g; Fat 11.2g, of which saturates 3.5g; Cholesterol 196mg; Calcium 65mg; Fibre 3.1g; Sodium 101mg.

# COURGETTE AND FETA PATTIES

*AT THEIR BEST WHEN COURGETTES ARE AT THEIR PEAK IN THE SUMMER, KABAK MUCVER MAKE A DELICIOUS SNACK OR HOT MEZE AT ANY TIME OF THE DAY. YOU COULD MAKE SMALLER ONES IF YOU ARE SERVING THE TASTY BITES WITH DRINKS. IF YOU LIKE A LITTLE FIRE ON YOUR TONGUE, ADD MORE TURKISH RED PEPPER OR CHILLIES TO THE MIXTURE.*

SERVES FOUR TO SIX

INGREDIENTS

3 firm courgettes (zucchini), washed
  and ends trimmed
30–45ml/2–3 tbsp olive oil
1 large onion, cut in half lengthways,
  in half again crossways, and sliced
  along the grain
4 garlic cloves, chopped
45ml/3 tbsp plain (all-purpose) flour
3 eggs, beaten
225g/8oz feta cheese, crumbled
1 bunch each of fresh flat leaf
  parsley, mint and dill, chopped
5ml/1 tsp kırmızı biber, or 1 fresh
  red chilli, seeded and chopped
sunflower oil, for shallow-frying
salt and ground black pepper
mint leaves, to garnish

1 Hold the courgettes at an angle and grate them, then put them in a sieve (strainer) and sprinkle with a little salt. Leave them to weep for 5 minutes.

2 Squeeze the grated courgettes in your hand to extract the juices. Heat the oil in a frying pan, stir in the courgettes, onion and garlic and fry until they begin to colour. Remove from the heat.

3 Transfer the flour to a bowl and beat in the eggs to form a smooth batter. Beat in the cooled courgette mixture. Add the feta, herbs and kırmızı biber or chilli, and season with black pepper. Add salt if you like, but usually the feta is quite salty. Mix well.

4 Heat enough sunflower oil for shallow-frying in a heavy, non-stick pan. Drop four spoonfuls of the mixture into the hot oil, leaving space between each one, then fry over a medium heat for 6–8 minutes, or until firm to the touch and golden brown on both sides.

5 Remove from the pan with a slotted spoon and drain on kitchen paper while you fry the remainder.

6 Serve while still warm, garnished with mint leaves.

Per portion Energy 327kcal/1354kJ; Protein 12.3g; Carbohydrate 12.4g, of which sugars 5.4g; Fat 25.7g, of which saturates 7.9g; Cholesterol 121mg; Calcium 214mg; Fibre 2.3g; Sodium 581mg.

# CARROT AND APRICOT ROLLS WITH MINT YOGURT

*THESE SWEET, HERBY CARROT ROLLS ARE A GREAT TREAT IN ISTANBUL AND IZMIR, BUT RARELY FOUND ELSEWHERE. SERVED WITH A DOLLOP OF YOGURT FLAVOURED WITH MINT AND GARLIC, THEY MAKE A DELICIOUS LIGHT LUNCH OR SUPPER WITH A GREEN SALAD AND WARM CRUSTY BREAD. ALTERNATIVELY, YOU CAN MOULD THE MIXTURE INTO MINIATURE BALLS AND SERVE THEM ON STICKS AS A NIBBLE TO GO WITH DRINKS, USING THE YOGURT AS A DIP.*

SERVES FOUR

INGREDIENTS
8–10 carrots, cut into thick slices
2–3 slices of day-old bread, ground
   into crumbs
4 spring onions (scallions),
   finely sliced
150g/5oz/generous ½ cup dried
   apricots, finely chopped or sliced
45ml/3 tbsp pine nuts
1 egg
5ml/1 tsp kırmızı biber, or
   1 fresh red chilli, seeded and
   finely chopped
1 bunch of fresh dill, chopped
1 bunch of fresh basil,
   finely shredded
salt and ground black pepper
plain (all-purpose) flour, for coating
sunflower oil, for shallow-frying
lemon wedges, to serve
For the mint yogurt
   about 225g/8oz/1 cup thick and
      creamy natural (plain) yogurt
   juice of ½ lemon
   1–2 garlic cloves, crushed
   1 bunch of fresh mint,
      finely chopped

**1** Steam the carrot slices for about 25 minutes, or until very soft. Do not boil them as they will will lose some of their flavour and natural sweetness.

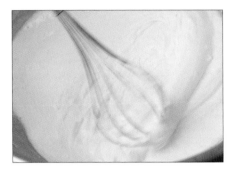

**2** Meanwhile, make the mint yogurt. Beat the yogurt in a bowl with the lemon juice and garlic, season with salt and pepper and stir in the mint. Set aside, or chill in the refrigerator.

**3** Mash the carrots to a paste while they are warm. Add the breadcrumbs, spring onions, apricots and pine nuts and mix well with a fork. Beat in the egg and stir in the kırmızı biber or chilli and herbs. Season with salt and pepper to taste.

**4** Put a small heap of flour on a flat surface. Take a plum-sized portion of the carrot mixture in your fingers and mould it into an oblong roll. If the mixture is very sticky, make it easier to deal with by adding more breadcrumbs or wetting your hands.

**5** Coat the carrot roll in the flour and put it on a plate. Repeat with rest of the mixture, to get 12–16 rolls altogether.

**6** Heat enough sunflower oil for shallow-frying in a heavy frying pan. Place the carrot rolls in the hot oil and fry over a medium heat for 8–10 minutes, turning them from time to time, until they are golden brown on all sides.

**7** Remove from the pan with a slotted spoon and drain on kitchen paper. Serve the rolls hot, with lemon wedges and the mint yogurt.

**VARIATIONS**
• You can make similar köfte (rolls) using the cooked flesh of sweet potatoes, combined with spices such as cinammon, ground cumin or kırmızı biber.
• Alternatively, shape the rolls from a mixture of plain mashed potato and lots of fresh herbs, such as flat leaf parsley or dill.

Per portion Energy 401kcal/1673kJ; Protein 8.7g; Carbohydrate 46g, of which sugars 29.1g; Fat 21.5g, of which saturates 2.5g; Cholesterol 48mg; Calcium 144mg; Fibre 8.5g; Sodium 145mg.

# CHICKPEA PATTIES WITH RED ONION AND PARSLEY

*THESE TASTY CUMIN-FLAVOURED PATTIES, CALLED NOHUTLU MÜCVER, CAN BE SERVED AS A SNACK OR AS PART OF A LIGHT MEAL WITH A CRUNCHY GREEN SALAD. MINI VERSIONS OF THE PATTIES ARE DELICIOUS STUFFED INTO PITTA BREAD POCKETS WITH LOTS OF RED ONION, FLAT LEAF PARSLEY AND A DRIZZLE OF YOGURT. EASY TO PREPARE, THEY CAN BE FRIED OR GRILLED AND CAN ALSO BE PREPARED AHEAD OF TIME AND KEPT IN THE REFRIGERATOR UNTIL REQUIRED.*

## SERVES FOUR

### INGREDIENTS
400g/14oz can chickpeas, drained
and thoroughly rinsed
45–60ml/3–4 tbsp olive oil
1 red onion, finely chopped
10ml/2 tsp cumin seeds, crushed
10ml/2 tsp ground coriander
5–10ml/1–2 tsp kırmızı biber,
or paprika
1 small bunch flat leaf parsley,
leaves finely chopped
1 small bunch dill, finely chopped
rind of 1 lemon
plain (all-purpose) flour, for dusting
salt and ground black pepper
To serve
45–60ml/3–4 tbsp thick and creamy
natural (plain) yogurt
1–2 garlic cloves, crushed
1 red onion, halved and sliced
1 small bunch flat leaf parsley,
leaves roughly chopped
1 lemon, sliced

**1** In a bowl, pound the chickpeas with a potato masher, or process them to a paste in a food processor or blender.

### COOK'S TIP
You could pound the chickpeas with the soaked bread, beans and the rest of the ingredients, then mould the mixture into balls to form köfte that are similar to the popular Middle Eastern falafel.

**2** Bind with 15ml/1 tbsp of the olive oil and beat in the onion, cumin, coriander, and kırmızı biber or paprika with a wooden spoon.

**3** Add the parsley, dill and lemon rind, and season the mixture with salt and pepper to taste.

**4** Mould portions of the chickpea mixture into small balls and flatten them in the palm of your hand to form thick patties (make these as big or as small as you like).

**5** Dust the patties in a little flour and fry them for 2 minutes on each side in the remaining olive oil in a non-stick pan. Drain them on kitchen paper.

**6** In a small bowl, beat the yogurt with the garlic, and season to taste.

**7** Arrange the patties on a large serving plate and serve them hot, or at room temperature, with the red onion, parsley, and lemon to squeeze over them, or a little garlic yogurt to drizzle over the top. Alternatively, you can tuck the patties into pitta pouches with the same ingredients.

**Per portion** Energy 246kcal/1032kJ; Protein 10.2g; Carbohydrate 24.7g, of which sugars 2.3g; Fat 12.8g, of which saturates 1.7g; Cholesterol 0mg; Calcium 118mg; Fibre 5.1g; Sodium 238mg.

# CHICKPEA PARCELS

*FALLING BETWEEN A CHINESE DUMPLING AND ITALIAN PASTA, BAKED MANTI IS A POPULAR SNACK IN
EASTERN ANATOLIA. THE CHICKPEA FILLING IS WARMING AND SATISFYING, MAKING IT PARTICULARLY
GOOD FOR VEGETARIANS. SERVE AS A HOT SNACK, OR AS A MEAL ON ITS OWN.*

**SERVES FOUR TO SIX**

INGREDIENTS
  450g/1lb/4 cups plain
    (all-purpose) flour
  2.5ml/½ tsp salt
  1 whole egg, beaten with 1 egg yolk
  salt and ground black pepper
For the filling
  400g/14oz can chickpeas, drained
    and thoroughly rinsed
  5ml/1 tsp cumin seeds, crushed
  5ml/1 tsp Turkish red pepper
    or paprika
For the yogurt
  about 90ml/6 tbsp thick and creamy
    natural (plain) yogurt
  2–3 garlic cloves, crushed
For the sauce
  15ml/1 tbsp olive oil
  15ml/1 tbsp butter
  1 onion, finely chopped
  2 garlic cloves, finely chopped
  5ml/1 tsp kırmızı biber, or
    1 fresh red chilli, seeded and
    finely chopped
  5–10ml/1–2 tsp sugar
  5–10ml/1–2 tsp dried mint
  400g/14oz can chopped tomatoes,
    drained of juice
  600ml/1 pint/2½ cups vegetable
    or chicken stock
  1 small bunch each of fresh flat leaf
    parsley and coriander (cilantro),
    roughly chopped

**1** Make the dough. Sift the flour and
salt into a wide bowl and make a well in
the middle. Pour in the beaten egg and
50ml/2fl oz/¼ cup water. Using your
fingers, draw the flour into the liquid
and mix to a dough.

**2** Knead the dough for 10 minutes,
cover the bowl with a damp dish towel
and leave the dough to rest for 1 hour.

**COOK'S TIP**
Manti can be baked or boiled, and the
fillings range from spicy minced (ground)
meat to chopped nuts or steamed spinach.

**3** Meanwhile, prepare the filling and
yogurt. In a bowl, mash the chickpeas
with a fork. Beat in the cumin, kırmızı
biber or paprika and seasoning.

**4** In a separate bowl, beat the yogurt
with the garlic and season with salt and
pepper to taste.

**5** Make the sauce. Heat the oil and
butter in a pan and gently fry the onion
and garlic until softened. Add the red
pepper or chilli, sugar and mint.

**6** Stir in the tomatoes and cook gently
over a low heat for about 15 minutes,
until the sauce is thick. Season and
remove from the heat.

**7** Preheat the oven to 200°C/400°F/
Gas 6. Roll out the dough as thinly as
possible on a lightly floured surface.
Using a sharp knife, cut the dough into
small squares (roughly 2.5cm/1in).

**8** Spoon a little chickpea mixture into
the middle of each square and bunch
together the corners to form a little
pouch. Place the filled pasta parcels
in a greased ovenproof dish, stacking
them next to each other. Bake,
uncovered, for 15–20 minutes, until
golden brown.

**9** Pour the stock into a pan and bring
to the boil. Take the parcels out of the
oven and pour the stock over them.

**10** Return the dish to the oven and
bake for a further 15–20 minutes, until
almost all the stock has been absorbed.
Meanwhile, reheat the tomato sauce.

**11** Transfer the pasta parcels to a
serving dish and spoon the yogurt over
them. Top the cool yogurt with the hot
tomato sauce and sprinkle with the
chopped herbs.

**Per portion** Energy 416kcal/1760kJ; Protein 14.8g; Carbohydrate 73.7g, of which sugars 5.9g; Fat 9g, of which saturates 2.6g; Cholesterol 71mg; Calcium 179mg; Fibre 5.9g; Sodium 360mg.

# FILO CIGARS FILLED WITH FETA, PARSLEY, MINT AND DILL

*These classic cigar-shaped pastries, sigara böreği, are a popular snack and meze food, and they are also good as nibbles with drinks. Here they are filled with a mixture of cheese and herbs, but other popular fillings include aromatic minced meat, baked aubergine and cheese, or mashed pumpkin, cheese and dill. The filo pastry can be folded into triangles, but cigars are the most traditional shape. They can be prepared in advance and kept under a damp dish towel in the refrigerator until you are ready to fry them.*

SERVES THREE TO FOUR

INGREDIENTS
  225g/8oz feta cheese
  1 large (US extra large) egg,
    lightly beaten
  1 small bunch each of fresh
    flat leaf parsley, mint and dill,
    finely chopped
  4–5 sheets of filo pastry
  sunflower oil, for deep-frying
  dill fronds, to garnish (optional)

**1** In a bowl, mash the feta with a fork. Beat in the egg and fold in the herbs.

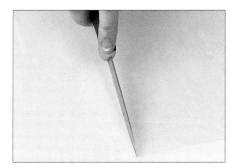

**2** Place the sheets of filo on a flat surface and cover with a damp dish towel to keep them moist. Working with one sheet at a time, cut the filo into strips about 10–13cm/4–5in wide, and pile them on top of each other. Keep the strips covered with another damp dish towel.

**3** Lay one filo strip on the surface in front of you, making sure you recover the other strips with the dish towel. Place a heaped teaspoon of the cheese filling along one of the short ends.

**4** Roll the end of the pastry over the filling, quite tightly to keep it in place, then tuck in the sides to seal in the filling and continue to roll until you get to the other end of the pastry.

**5** As you reach the end, load the tip of the brush with a little water and brush it over the end of the pastry – this will help seal the filo and prevent it unravelling during cooking.

**6** Place the filled filo pastry cigar, join-side down, on a plate and cover with another damp dish towel to keep it moist. Continue with the remaining sheets of filo and filling until all the filling has been used.

**7** Heat enough oil for deep-frying in a wok or other deep-sided pan, and deep-fry the filo cigars in batches for 5–6 minutes until crisp and golden brown. Lift out of the oil with a slotted spoon and drain on kitchen paper.

**8** Serve immediately, garnished with dill fronds if you like.

### VARIATION
To make a puff pastry log, use the same filling as here. Roll out a 400g/14oz packet puff pastry and spoon on the filling. Roll into a log, tucking in the ends as you go, and place on an oiled baking tray. Cut diagonally into portions, keeping it intact at the base. Brush with a mixture of egg yolk and sunflower oil and bake in a preheated oven at 180°C/350°F/Gas 4 for 30 minutes, until crisp.

**Per portion** Energy 311kcal/1291kJ; Protein 12.4g; Carbohydrate 11.2g, of which sugars 1.6g; Fat 24.4g, of which saturates 9.5g; Cholesterol 92mg; Calcium 278mg; Fibre 1.6g; Sodium 838mg.

# SNACKS

*Savoury and sweet snacks are essentially more substantial*

*forms of meze. They range from treats like Deep-fried Mussels*

*in Beer Batter to flatbreads rolled with spinach or meat and*

*a sustaining Layered Mince Meat and Pine Nut Pie. Sweet*

*pastries, such as Baklava, Ladies' Navels and Cheese-filled*

*Pastry in Lemon Syrup are extremely popular at any time*

*of the day, as are the various fruit jams that are enjoyed*

*with bread and cheese.*

# ANATOLIAN FLAT BREADS WITH SPINACH

*THESE TRADITIONAL FLAT BREADS FROM CENTRAL ANATOLIA, CALLED GÖZLEME, ARE COOKED QUICKLY ON A HOT GRIDDLE AND CAN BE FILLED WITH VARIOUS COMBINATIONS OF INGREDIENTS, INCLUDING CHEESE AND HERBS, EGGS AND PASTIRMA, MINCED BEEF WITH PINE NUTS, OR WITH THIS CREAMY SPINACH AND ONION MIXTURE. FOR BREAKFAST, THEY ARE OFTEN COOKED PLAIN AND DRIZZLED WITH JUST A LITTLE HONEY. GREAT AS A SNACK, OR AS A LIGHT LUNCH, THIS IS A TRADITIONAL VILLAGE DISH THAT IS PREPARED IN THE HOME AND IN SMALL CAFÉS AND RESTAURANTS.*

SERVES TWO TO FOUR

INGREDIENTS

115g/4oz/1 cup strong unbleached
   white bread flour, plus extra
   for dusting
2.5ml/½ tsp salt
15ml/1 tbsp olive oil, melted
   butter or ghee
50ml/2fl oz/¼ cup water
For the filling
250g/9oz fresh spinach
15g/½ oz/1 tbsp butter
1 onion, chopped
pinch of freshly grated nutmeg
5ml/1 tsp kırmızı biber,
   or paprika
7.5ml/1½ tsp plain
   (all-purpose) flour
120ml/4fl oz/½ cup milk
45ml/3 tbsp kaşar peynir or
   Parmesan cheese, grated
salt and ground black pepper

**1** Sift the flour with the salt into a bowl. Make a well in the centre and pour in the oil, or melted butter or ghee, and the water. Using your hand, draw in the flour from the sides and work the mixture into a dough. Knead thoroughly.

**2** Divide the dough into four pieces, knead them and roll into balls. Place the balls on a floured surface, cover with a damp cloth, and leave them to rest for 30 minutes.

**3** Meanwhile, prepare the filling. Place the spinach in a steamer, or in a colander set in a large pan with a lid, and steam the spinach until it wilts.

**4** Refresh the spinach under running cold water and drain well. Place the cooked spinach on a wooden board and chop it roughly.

**5** Melt the butter in a heavy pan and soften the onion. Stir in the chopped spinach and add the nutmeg and kırmızı biber or paprika.

**6** Stir in the flour and pour in the milk, stirring constantly until thickened. Beat in the cheese and season with salt and pepper. Cover the pan to keep the filling warm.

**7** On a lightly floured surface, roll out each of the balls of dough with a rolling pin into thin, flat rounds, about 15–20cm/6–8in in diameter.

**8** Heat a griddle, wipe it with a little oil, and place one of the rounds of dough on to it (if you have a wide griddle, as they do in Turkey, you can cook several at a time). Cook the dough for about 1 minute on one side, then flip it over and spread a thin layer of the spinach filling over the cooked side.

**9** Cook the second side for 1–2 minutes, allowing it to buckle and brown, then lift it off the griddle and place it on a piece of baking parchment.

**10** Roll up the gözleme, wrap the paper around it to make it easier to hold, and hand it to the first person waiting to try one before repeating with the others.

**VARIATION**
An alternative method is to spread the filling on one half of the cooking gözleme and fold the other half over to resemble a half moon. Make sure the edges are sealed and serve immediately.

**Per portion** Energy 246kcal/1033kJ; Protein 10.5g; Carbohydrate 27.9g, of which sugars 3.7g; Fat 11.1g, of which saturates 5.1g; Cholesterol 21mg; Calcium 327mg; Fibre 2.5g; Sodium 493mg.

# COURGETTE FRITTERS

*OFTEN SERVED AS A HOT MEZE DISH, KABAK KIZARTMASI ARE DELICIOUS SERVED WITH YOGURT, WHICH CAN BE PLAIN OR FLAVOURED WITH GARLIC, AS HERE. THEY ARE ALSO TASTY SERVED WITH LEMON WEDGES TO SQUEEZE OVER THEM, AND ARE EQUALLY GOOD AS A QUICK SNACK OR AS A LIGHT LUNCH WITH A SALAD. VARIATIONS OF THESE FRITTERS ARE COOKED ALL OVER TURKEY.*

SERVES FOUR

INGREDIENTS
   3–4 firm, fat courgettes
    (zucchini)
   2 eggs
   30ml/2 tbsp plain
    (all-purpose) flour
   sunflower oil, for deep-frying
   salt and ground black pepper
To serve
   60ml/4 tbsp thick and creamy
    natural (plain) yogurt
   1 garlic clove, crushed
   juice of ½ lemon

**1** Cut the courgettes on the diagonal, crossways, into thin slices. If moist, pat them dry with a piece of kitchen paper, so that the batter will stick to them.

**2** Beat the eggs in a bowl and add the flour. Beat until smooth and season with salt and pepper.

**3** Heat enough oil for deep-frying in a wide, shallow pan. Dip the courgette slices into the batter and then drop them into the oil. Fry them in batches for 3–4 minutes, or until golden brown all over. Drain the fritters on kitchen paper and keep warm.

**4** In a small bowl, quickly beat the yogurt with the garlic and lemon juice. Season to taste.

**5** Arrange the warm fritters on a serving dish with the yogurt. Enjoy the juicy fritters dipped in the garlic yogurt as a snack or as a hot meze dish.

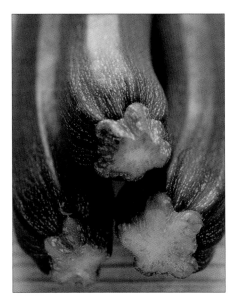

**Per portion** Energy 207kcal/857kJ; Protein 8.3g; Carbohydrate 10.8g, of which sugars 4.7g; Fat 14.8g, of which saturates 2.4g; Cholesterol 95mg; Calcium 104mg; Fibre 2.1g; Sodium 50mg.

# STIR-FRIED SPINACH WITH CURRANTS

*THERE ARE ENDLESS VERSIONS OF TRADITIONAL SPINACH AND YOGURT MEZE DISHES AND SNACKS, RANGING FROM PLAIN STEAMED SPINACH SERVED WITH YOGURT, TO THIS SWEET AND TANGY ANATOLIAN CREATION, WHICH IS TAMED WITH GARLIC-FLAVOURED YOGURT. SERVE THIS DISH WHILE IT IS STILL WARM, WITH WARM FLAT BREAD OR CHUNKS OF A CRUSTY LOAF TO ACCOMPANY IT.*

SERVES THREE TO FOUR

INGREDIENTS
  350g/12oz fresh spinach leaves,
    thoroughly washed and drained
  about 200g/7oz/scant 1 cup
    thick and creamy natural
    (plain) yogurt
  2 garlic cloves, crushed
  30–45ml/2–3 tbsp olive oil
  1 red onion, cut in half lengthways,
    in half again crossways, and sliced
    along the grain
  5ml/1 tsp sugar
  15–30ml/1–2 tbsp currants, soaked
    in warm water for 5–10 minutes
    and drained
  30ml/2 tbsp pine nuts
  5–10ml/1–2 tsp kırmızı biber,
    or 1 fresh red chilli, seeded
    and finely chopped
  juice of 1 lemon
  salt and ground black pepper
  a pinch of paprika,
    to garnish

**1** Steam the spinach for 3–4 minutes, until wilted and soft. Drain off any excess water and chop the spinach.

**2** In a bowl, beat the yogurt with the garlic. Season and set aside.

**VARIATION**
To make a simple spinach and yogurt dish, steam the spinach until soft, then chop it to a pulp. Mix the yogurt with a finely chopped clove of garlic and beat in the spinach. Season and serve.

**3** Heat the olive oil in a heavy pan and gently fry the onion and sugar, stirring, until the onion begins to colour. Add the currants, pine nuts and kırmızı biber or chilli and fry until the nuts just begin to colour.

**4** Add the spinach, tossing it around the pan until everything is well mixed, then pour in the lemon juice and season with salt and pepper.

**5** Serve the spinach straight from the pan with the yogurt spooned on top, or tip into a serving dish and make a well in the middle, then spoon the yogurt into the well, drizzling some of it over the spinach. Serve hot, sprinkled with a little paprika.

Per portion Energy 145kcal/603kJ; Protein 5.8g; Carbohydrate 10.2g, of which sugars 9.8g; Fat 9.3g, of which saturates 1.3g; Cholesterol 1mg; Calcium 252mg; Fibre 2.2g; Sodium 165mg.

# DEEP-FRIED SQUID <u>WITH</u> GARLIC BREAD SAUCE

*KALAMAR — DEEP-FRIED SQUID — IS OFTEN SERVED AS A HOT MEZE DISH IN FISH RESTAURANTS, AND IN SOME COASTAL AREAS IT WILL BE OFFERED TO YOU AS A SNACK TO ACCOMPANY A CHILLED GLASS OF BEER OR RAKI. CUT INTO RINGS OR STRIPS, THE SQUID IS GENERALLY SERVED WITH LEMON TO SQUEEZE OVER IT, A DILL-FLAVOURED MAYONNAISE, OR A GARLIC AND NUT OR BREAD SAUCE. THE MOST TRADITIONAL VERSION, WHICH IS MOST FREQUENTLY SERVED IN THE MAKESHIFT STALLS AND FISH LOKANTAS, IS THIS SIMPLE ONE MADE WITH BREAD. THE SQUID CAN BE SIMPLY TOSSED IN FLOUR BEFORE FRYING, OR DIPPED INTO A YEAST AND BEER BATTER, AS HERE.*

## SERVES TWO TO FOUR

### INGREDIENTS

4 good-sized fresh squid, prepared
 (*see* Cook's Tip)
sunflower oil, for deep-frying
1 lemon, cut into wedges,
 to serve

For the batter
15g/½ oz fresh yeast
300ml/½ pint/1¼ cups beer
225g/8oz plain (all-purpose) flour
5ml/1 tsp salt

For the sauce
3 slices day-old white bread,
 with crusts removed
100ml/3½ fl oz/scant ½ cup
 olive oil
juice of 1 lemon
2–3 garlic cloves, crushed
salt and ground black pepper

**1** Cut the prepared squid into strips or rings and set aside.

**2** To make the batter, cream the yeast with 30ml/2 tbsp of the beer in a small bowl. Gradually stir in the remainder of the beer. Sift the flour with the salt into a bowl.

**3** Make a well in the centre of the flour and pour in the beer and yeast mixture, beating constantly. Use a whisk to produce a smooth batter, then cover it and leave to stand for 1 hour.

**4** To make the sauce, soak the bread in water for 10 minutes. Squeeze it dry and put it in a bowl.

**5** Using a fork, or a wooden spoon, beat the oil and lemon juice with the bread until it resembles a thick sauce.

**6** Beat in the garlic and season with salt and pepper. Transfer to a serving bowl and set aside.

**7** Heat enough oil for deep-frying in a pan. Dip the squid in the batter and fry it in batches. When the batter turns crisp and golden brown, lift the squid out of the oil and place the fried pieces on a trivet in the pan to keep them warm while you fry the remaining squid. When all of the squid has been cooked, drain on kitchen paper.

**8** Serve hot with the garlic sauce and lemon to squeeze over it.

### COOK'S TIPS

• **Preparing the squid** First, hold the body sac in one hand and pull the head off with the other. Most of the innards should come out with the head, but reach inside the sac with your fingers to remove any that remain. Remove the transparent backbone and rinse the body sac inside and out. Pat the body sac dry and put it aside for stuffing. Sever the tentacles just above the eyes, so that you have the top of the head and the tentacles joined together. Put them aside with the sacs and discard everything else.

• **Tenderizing tip** To soften the squid and draw out its taste, some Turkish cooks rub it in lemon juice, sprinkle a little sugar over it with a teaspoon of bicarbonate of soda and chill it in the refrigerator for an hour. The squid is then rinsed and patted dry before cooking.

**Per portion** Energy 636kcal/2668kJ; Protein 34g; Carbohydrate 56.2g, of which sugars 2.5g; Fat 31g, of which saturates 4.5g; Cholesterol 394mg; Calcium 126mg; Fibre 2g; Sodium 296mg.

# DEEP-FRIED MUSSELS IN BEER BATTER

*FRIED IN HUGE, CURVED PANS, MIDYE TAVASI ARE SKEWERED ON STICKS AND SOLD IN BATCHES, WITH A GARLIC-FLAVOURED TARATOR SAUCE THAT CAN BE MADE WITH POUNDED WALNUTS, ALMONDS OR PINE NUTS, OR SIMPLY WITH DAY-OLD BREAD. A SPECIALITY FROM ISTANBUL AND IZMIR, THEY ARE PART OF THE STREET-FOOD SCENE, AS WELL AS BEING POPULAR IN FISH RESTAURANTS.*

**3** Drizzle in the olive oil, stirring all the time, and beat in the lemon juice and vinegar. The sauce should be smooth, with the consistency of thick cream – if it is too dry, stir in a little water. Season with salt and pepper and set aside.

**4** Heat enough sunflower oil for deep-frying in a large wok or other large, heavy pan.

**5** Using your fingers, dip each mussel into the batter and drop into the hot oil. Fry in batches for a minute or two until golden brown. Lift out with a slotted spoon and drain well on kitchen paper.

**6** Thread the mussels on to wooden skewers, or spear them individually, and serve hot, accompanied by the garlic-flavoured dipping sauce.

**COOK'S TIP**
Raw mussels are prised from their shells with ease by the street vendors, but an easier option is to steam them open for 3–4 minutes, then remove them from their shells.

## SERVES FOUR TO FIVE

INGREDIENTS
  sunflower oil, for deep-frying
  about 50 fresh mussels, cleaned,
    shelled and patted dry (*see* below)
For the batter
  115g/4oz/1 cup plain (all-purpose) flour
  5ml/1 tsp salt
  2.5ml/½ tsp bicarbonate of soda
    (baking soda)
  2 egg yolks
  175–250ml/6–8fl oz/¾–1 cup beer
For the sauce
  75g/3oz/½ cup shelled walnuts
  2 slices of day-old bread, sprinkled
    with water and left for a few
    minutes, then squeezed dry
  2–3 garlic cloves, crushed
  45–60ml/3–4 tbsp olive oil
  juice of 1 lemon
  dash of white wine vinegar
  salt and ground black pepper

**1** Make the batter. Sift the flour, salt and soda into a bowl. Make a well in the middle and drop in the egg yolks. Beat in the beer and draw in the flour from the sides until a smooth, thick batter is formed. Set aside for 30 minutes.

**2** Meanwhile, make the sauce. Pound the walnuts to a paste using a mortar and pestle, or blend them in a processor. Add the bread and garlic, and pound again to a paste.

**Per portion** Energy 439kcal/1827kJ; Protein 10.6g; Carbohydrate 24.6g, of which sugars 1.9g; Fat 33g, of which saturates 4g; Cholesterol 89mg; Calcium 115mg; Fibre 1.5g; Sodium 502mg.

# ANCHOVIES POACHED <u>IN</u> VINE LEAVES

*STREET VENDORS IN CITIES PREPARE LARGE PANS OF THESE POACHED ANCHOVIES — HAMSI SARMASI — WHICH CAN BE EASILY EATEN WITH THE FINGERS, AS THE WRAPPED FISH IS SIMPLY POPPED INTO THE MOUTH AND EATEN WHOLE. THIS IS A VERY POPULAR DISH IN THE EARLY WEEKS OF SUMMER, WHEN THE ANCHOVIES ARE SWEET AND JUICY AND THE VINE LEAVES TENDER.*

SERVES FOUR TO SIX

INGREDIENTS
about 24 fresh anchovies, gutted and
cleaned, with the backbone removed
about 24 fresh or preserved vine
leaves, plus extra for lining the pan
60ml/4 tbsp olive oil
juice of 1 lemon
1–2 garlic cloves, crushed (optional)
salt and ground black pepper
To serve
1 lemon, cut into thick slices
5–10ml/1–2 tsp sumac

**4** Place a plate directly on top of the wrapped anchovies to keep them in place while cooking. Cover the pan and poach the anchovies gently for 10 minutes.

**5** Arrange the anchovies on a serving dish with the lemon slices. Sprinkle a little sumac over the top of the fish and eat them whole while still hot, or at room temperature.

**1** Place the anchovies on a flat surface and wrap them in the vine leaves with their heads poking out.

**2** Line a shallow pan with a few of the extra vine leaves and place the wrapped anchovies on top, packing them together quite tightly.

**3** Mix the olive oil and lemon juice together, beat in the garlic, if using, and salt and pepper. Pour the mixture over the anchovies.

**Per portion** Energy 190kcal/788kJ; Protein 14.4g; Carbohydrate 2.5g, of which sugars 2.5g; Fat 13.6g, of which saturates 2.9g; Cholesterol 0mg; Calcium 81mg; Fibre 1.1g; Sodium 84mg.

# FLATBREADS <u>WITH</u> SPICY LAMB <u>AND</u> TOMATO

*This Anatolian snack, lahmacun, is a great culinary creation. The thin crispy base is smeared with a layer of lightly spiced lamb and rolled into a cone with fresh parsley, sumac and a squeeze of lemon. It is the most perfect form of street food — hot, portable and delicious. In restaurants, miniature versions are often served as a hot meze dish.*

SERVES TWO TO FOUR

INGREDIENTS
  scant 5ml/1 tsp active dried yeast
  2.5ml/½ tsp sugar
  150ml/¼ pint/⅔ cup lukewarm water
  350g/12oz/3 cups strong white
    bread flour
  2.5ml/½ tsp salt
  a few drops of sunflower oil
For the topping
  15ml/1 tbsp olive oil
  15ml/1 tbsp butter
  1 onion, finely chopped
  2 garlic cloves, finely chopped
  225g/8oz/1 cup finely minced
    (ground) lean lamb
  30ml/2 tbsp tomato purée (paste)
  15ml/1 tbsp sugar
  5–10ml/1–2 tsp kırmızı biber, or
    1 fresh red chilli, finely chopped
  5ml/1 tsp dried mint
  5–10ml/1–2 tsp ground sumac
  1 bunch of fresh flat leaf parsley,
    roughly chopped
  1 lemon, halved
  salt and ground black pepper

**1** Make the dough. Put the yeast and sugar into a small bowl with half the lukewarm water. Set aside for about 15 minutes until frothy.

**2** Sift the flour and salt into a large bowl, make a well in the middle and add the creamed yeast and the rest of the lukewarm water. Using your hand, draw in the flour and work the mixture to a dough, adding more water if necessary.

**3** Turn the dough on to a lightly floured surface and knead until it is smooth and elastic. Drip a few drops of sunflower oil into the base of the bowl and roll the dough in it. Cover the bowl with a damp dish towel and leave in a warm place for about 1 hour or until the dough has doubled in size.

**4** Meanwhile, prepare the topping. Heat the oil and butter in a heavy pan and gently fry the onion and garlic until they soften. Leave to cool in the pan.

**5** Put the lamb in a bowl, add the tomato purée, sugar, kırmızı biber or chilli and mint, then the softened onion and garlic. Season with salt and pepper, and knead with your hands. Cover and keep in the refrigerator until you are ready to use.

**6** Place two baking sheets in the oven. Preheat the oven to 220°C/425°F/Gas 7. Punch down the risen dough, knead it on a lightly floured surface, then divide into two or four equal pieces. Roll each piece into a thin flat round, stretching the dough with your hands as you roll.

**7** Oil the hot baking sheets and place the dough rounds on them, then cover with a thin layer of the meat mixture, spreading it right to the edges. Bake in the oven for 15–20 minutes, until the meat is nicely cooked.

**8** As soon as the lahmacun are ready, sprinkle them with the sumac and parsley. Squeeze a little lemon juice over the top and roll them up while the dough is still pliable. Eat like a pizza – with your hands, or on plates with a knife and fork.

**Per portion** Energy 496kcal/2092kJ; Protein 20g; Carbohydrate 75.2g, of which sugars 8.1g; Fat 14.9g, of which saturates 6.1g; Cholesterol 51mg; Calcium 167mg; Fibre 3.8g; Sodium 333mg.

# LAYERED MINCED MEAT AND PINE NUT PIE

*A TEPSI IS A DEEP ROUND BAKING TRAY IN WHICH SAVOURY AND SWEET PASTRIES ARE BAKED. IN THIS DISH, TEPSI BÖREĞI, THE SHEETS OF TRADITIONAL FLAT BREAD, YUFKA, ARE LAYERED WITH A MINCED MEAT FILLING. ALTHOUGH NOT EXACTLY THE SAME, FILO PASTRY, WHICH IS MORE READILY AVAILABLE, WORKS AS A SUBSTITUTE FOR THE LARGE SHEETS OF TRADITIONAL YUFKA, BUT YOU MAY REQUIRE TWICE AS MANY SHEETS OF FILO, AS THEY ARE USUALLY SMALLER IN SIZE.*

SERVES FOUR TO SIX

INGREDIENTS
  2 eggs
  300ml/½ pint/1¼ cups milk
  150ml/¼ pint/⅔ cup sunflower oil
    or olive oil, plus 15ml/1 tbsp extra
  5 sheets of yufka or 10–12 of filo
    pastry, thawed if frozen
For the filling
  15ml/1 tbsp olive oil
  15g/½oz/1 tbsp butter
  1 onion, finely chopped
  2–3 garlic cloves, crushed
  30–45ml/2–3 tbsp pine nuts
  250g/9oz lean veal or beef, finely
    minced (ground)
  10ml/2 tsp ground cinnamon
  10ml/2 tsp dried oregano
  1 small bunch fresh parsley, leaves
    finely chopped
  salt and ground black pepper
To serve
  7.5ml/1½ tsp olive oil or butter
  15ml/1 tbsp pine nuts

**1** Preheat the oven to 200°C/400°F/ Gas 6 and grease an ovenproof dish (the size is not important – just vary the number of layers according to the dish).

**2** For the filling, heat the olive oil and butter in a heavy pan and stir in the onion. Cook for 1–2 minutes until softened. Add the garlic and pine nuts. Once the pine nuts begin to turn golden, add the meat.

**3** Cook the meat for 3–4 minutes, then stir in the cinnamon and herbs. Season with salt and pepper. Leave to cool.

**4** In a bowl, beat the eggs with the milk and the oil. Lay a whole sheet of yufka in the base of the dish, with the sides overlapping the edge – this may require two to three sheets of filo pastry, overlapped in the base of the dish to prevent seepage. (If using filo, keep the unused pastry covered with a damp dish towel to prevent drying.)

**5** Pour a little of the milk mixture into the centre and spread it to the sides.

**6** Tear two sheets of yufka (or three to four of filo) into wide strips and layer them in the dish, brushing each layer with the milk mixture. Leave the last layer dry and spread the meat mixture over it.

**7** Tear the remaining two sheets of yufka (three to four of filo) and layer them up in the same way with the milk mixture. Reserve 15ml/1 tbsp of the mixture in the bowl and beat in the 15ml/1 tbsp of the oil.

**8** Pull up the dangling flaps of yufka from the base sheet lining the dish and fold them over the top of the pie, sticking them down with the milk and oil mixture, which you can apply with a brush, but it is easier and more effective to smear it on with your fingers.

**9** Make sure the very top pieces are well oiled, and put the pie into the oven for about 45 minutes. The pie should puff up and turn golden brown.

**10** Remove the pie from the oven (it will sink back down quite quickly) and cut it into rectangular, square or triangular wedges, according to your preference.

**11** To serve, heat the oil or butter in a small pan, add the pine nuts and cook until golden brown. Drain them on kitchen paper and sprinkle a few over each portion. Serve the pie hot or at room temperature.

**Per portion** Energy 463kcal/1920kJ; Protein 15.1g; Carbohydrate 16.5g, of which sugars 3.6g; Fat 37.9g, of which saturates 8.1g; Cholesterol 97mg; Calcium 101mg; Fibre 0.9g; Sodium 94mg.

# CHEESE-FILLED PASTRY IN LEMON SYRUP

*THIS DELECTABLE SWEET PASTRY, KÜNEFE, IS MADE WITH THE THIN STRANDS OF PASTRY THAT MANY VISITORS TO TURKEY REFER TO AS 'SHREDDED WHEAT'. DIFFICULT TO MAKE AT HOME, AS THE BATTER REQUIRES TOSSING THROUGH A STRAINER ON TO A HOT METAL SHEET OVER AN OPEN FIRE, THE PASTRY IS AVAILABLE READY PREPARED IN MOST MIDDLE EASTERN AND TURKISH FOOD STORES — LOOK FOR PACKS OF PALE STRANDS THAT LOOK LIKE VERMICELLI AND ARE CALLED KADAYIF. SOMETIMES THIS SWEET PASTRY IS SIMPLY CALLED KADAYIF BECAUSE OF THE TYPE OF PASTRY USED.*

### SERVES SIX

### INGREDIENTS

225g/8oz ready-prepared kadayif
  pastry, thawed if frozen, shredded
115g/4oz clarified butter,
  or ghee, melted
350g/12oz dil peyniri,
  or mozzarella, sliced
15–30ml/1–2 tbsp pistachio nuts,
  coarsely chopped
For the syrup
225g/8oz/generous 1 cup sugar
120ml/4fl oz/½ cup water
juice of 1 lemon

**1** Preheat oven to 180°C/350°F/Gas 4. To make the syrup, put the sugar and water into a pan and bring it to the boil, stirring with a wooden spoon until the sugar has dissolved.

**2** Add the lemon juice, reduce the heat, and simmer for 15 minutes, until it coats the back of the wooden spoon.

**3** Turn off the heat and leave the syrup to cool. Chill it in the refrigerator until needed, if you like.

**4** Put the shredded pastry into a bowl and separate the strands.

**5** Pour the clarified butter or melted ghee over them and, using your fingers, rub it all over the strands so that they are completely coated in it.

**6** Spread half the pastry in the base of a baking tin (pan) (the Turks use a round tin about 27cm/10½in in diameter), and press it down with your fingers.

**7** Lay the slices of cheese over the top of the pastry and cover with the remainder of the pastry, pressing it down firmly and tucking it down the sides of the baking tin.

**8** Place the pastry in the oven for about 45 minutes, or until it is golden brown.

**9** Remove from the oven and leave to cool slightly for 10 minutes.

**10** Loosen the edges of the pastry with a sharp knife and pour the cold syrup over it. Sprinkle the pistachio nuts over the top.

**11** Divide the pastry into squares or segments, depending on the shape of your baking tin, and serve while it is still warm.

### COOK'S TIPS

• The same pastry is used to make kiz memesi kadayif – 'young girls' breasts' – a great favourite of the Ottoman Palace kitchens. Traditionally, the pastry chefs made these filled shredded pastries in special, individual, non-stick pans cooked on the stove, but the homemade version is baked in the oven.
• The cheese most commonly used for the filling is the elastic dil peyniri, which peels off in threads, but the blocks of hard mozzarella used for pizzas are very similar in texture and taste.

**Per portion** Energy 595kcal/2486kJ; Protein 13.7g; Carbohydrate 53.4g, of which sugars 39.9g; Fat 38.2g, of which saturates 18.2g; Cholesterol 75mg; Calcium 259mg; Fibre 0.2g; Sodium 478mg.

# YOGURT CAKE IN ORANGE SYRUP

*THERE ARE MANY VERSIONS OF THIS YOGURT CAKE OR DESSERT, CALLED YOĞURT TATLISI. SOME INCLUDE COCONUT, SULTANAS OR GROUND WALNUTS, SERVED AS A CAKE WITH A GLASS OF TEA, WHEREAS OTHER VERSIONS ARE SOAKED IN SYRUP AND ENJOYED AS A SWEET SNACK OR DESSERT.*

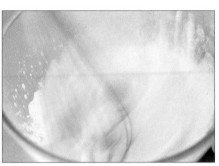

**2** In a bowl, beat the eggs with the sugar until light and fluffy. Beat in the flour, then the yogurt, lemon rind and lemon juice.

**3** Transfer the mixture to the prepared tin or dish and pop it in the oven for about 45 minutes. The cake should rise and turn golden brown on top.

**4** Meanwhile, prepare the syrup. Heat the sugar and water in a heavy pan, stirring constantly, until the sugar has dissolved. Stir in the orange juice and orange rind and bring the liquid to the boil. Reduce the heat and simmer for 10–15 minutes. Leave the syrup to cool.

**5** When the cake is ready, turn it out on to a serving dish and pour the cold syrup over it. Serve warm or at room temperature on its own, or with kaymak (clotted cream).

## SERVES SIX

### INGREDIENTS
  4 eggs
  115g/4oz/generous ½ cup sugar
  115g/4oz self-raising
   (self-rising) flour
  400g/14oz tub of thick and creamy
   natural (plain) yogurt, strained
  grated rind of 1 lemon
  juice of 1 lemon
For the syrup
  225g/8oz/generous 1 cup sugar
  120ml/4fl oz/½ cup water
  juice of 1 orange
  rind of 1 orange, finely shredded

**1** Preheat the oven to 180°C/350°F/Gas 4. Prepare a baking tin (pan) or dish (the Turks use a round tepsi approximately 23cm/9in in diameter) by greasing it lightly with oil or butter.

### COOK'S TIP
The Turkish rule with all their syrupy pastries and sponges is that if the pudding is hot, the syrup should be cold, even chilled, and vice versa.

**Per portion** Energy 415kcal/1757kJ; Protein 10.5g; Carbohydrate 75.8g, of which sugars 61.5g; Fat 10.7g, of which saturates 4.5g; Cholesterol 127mg; Calcium 217mg; Fibre 0.6g; Sodium 167mg.

# LADIES' NAVELS

*THIS CLASSIC FRIED PASTRY, KADIN GÖBEĞI, IS AN INVENTION FROM THE TOPKAPI PALACE KITCHENS. GARNISH IT WITH WHOLE OR CHOPPED PISTACHIO NUTS AND SERVE WITH KAYMAK (THICK BUFFALO CREAM), OR ANY OTHER CREAM YOU LIKE, AS A DELICIOUS HOT SNACK OR DESSERT.*

SERVES FOUR TO SIX

INGREDIENTS
    50g/2oz/¼ cup butter
    2.5ml/½ tsp salt
    175g/6oz/1½ cups plain
     (all-purpose) flour
    60g/2oz/⅓ cup semolina
    2 eggs
    sunflower oil, for deep-frying
For the syrup
    450g/1lb/scant 2¼ cups sugar
    juice of 1 lemon

**1** Make the sugar syrup. Put the sugar and 300ml/½ pint/1¼ cups water into a large, heavy pan and bring to the boil, stirring all the time. When the sugar has dissolved completely, stir in the lemon juice and lower the heat, then simmer for about 10 minutes, until the syrup has thickened a little. Remove from the heat and leave to cool.

**2** Put the butter, salt and 250ml/8fl oz/ 1 cup water in another heavy pan and bring to the boil. Remove from the heat and add the flour and semolina, beating all the time, until the mixture becomes smooth and leaves the side of the pan. Leave to cool.

**3** Beat the eggs into the cooled mixture so that it gleams. Add 15ml/1 tbsp of the cooled syrup and beat well.

**4** Pour enough oil for deep-frying into a wok or deep-sided pan. Heat until warm, then remove from the heat.

**5** Wet your hands and take an apricot-size piece of dough in your fingers. Roll it into a ball, flatten it in the palm of your hand, then use your finger to make an indentation in the middle to resemble a lady's navel.

**6** Drop the balls of dough into the pan of warmed oil. Repeat with the rest of the mixture to make about 12 navels.

**7** Place the pan back over the heat. As the oil heats up, the pastries will swell, retaining the dip in the middle. Swirl the oil, until the navels turn golden all over.

**8** Remove the navels from the oil with a slotted spoon, then toss them in the cooled syrup. Leave to soak for a few minutes, arrange in a serving dish and spoon some of the syrup over.

Per portion Energy 517kcal/2190kJ; Protein 6.3g; Carbohydrate 108.8g, of which sugars 78.9g; Fat 9.3g, of which saturates 4.9g; Cholesterol 81mg; Calcium 93mg; Fibre 1.1g; Sodium 80mg.

# BAKLAVA

*AN OTTOMAN LEGACY, BAKLAVA IS ONE OF THE GREATEST CREATIONS FROM THE PASTRY CHEFS AT THE TOPKAPI PALACE. TRADITIONALLY MADE WITH EIGHT LAYERS OF PASTRY DOUGH AND SEVEN LAYERS OF CHOPPED NUTS, THE SECRET IS SAID TO BE IN THE SPECIALLY PREPARED, PAPER-THIN DOUGH MADE FROM CLARIFIED BUTTER AND THE FINEST FLOUR. BAKLAVA IS ENJOYED AS A MID-MORNING SWEET SNACK WITH A CUP OF TURKISH COFFEE, OR AS A MID-AFTERNOON PICK-ME-UP WITH A GLASS OF TEA.*

SERVES TWELVE

INGREDIENTS
  175g/6oz/¾ cup clarified or plain
    butter, or sunflower oil
  100ml/3½fl oz/scant ½ cup
    sunflower oil
  450g/1lb filo sheets
  450g/1lb walnuts, or a mixture of
    walnuts, pistachios and almonds,
    finely chopped
  5ml/1 tsp ground cinnamon
For the syrup
  450g/1lb sugar
  juice of 1 lemon, or 30ml/2 tbsp
    rose water

**1** Preheat the oven to 160°C/325°F/ Gas 3. Melt the butter and oil in a small pan, then brush a little over the bottom and sides of a 30cm/12in round or square cake tin (pan).

**2** Place a sheet of filo in the bottom and brush it with melted butter and oil. Continue until you have used half the filo sheets, brushing each one with butter and oil. Ease the sheets into the corners and trim the edges if they flop over the rim of the tin.

**3** Spread the nuts over the last buttered sheet and sprinkle with the cinnamon, then continue as before with the remaining filo sheets. Brush the top one as well, then, using a sharp knife, cut diagonal parallel lines right through all the layers to the bottom to form small diamond shapes.

**4** Bake the baklava in the oven for about 1 hour, until the top is golden – if it is still pale, increase the temperature for a few minutes at the end.

**5** While the baklava is in the oven, make the syrup. Put the sugar into a medium, heavy pan, pour in 250ml/8fl oz/1 cup water and bring the mixture to the boil, stirring constantly.

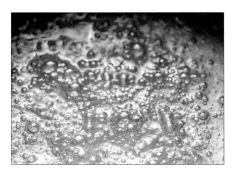

**6** When the sugar has dissolved, lower the heat and stir in the lemon juice, then simmer for 15 minutes, until the syrup thickens. Leave to cool in the pan.

**7** Remove from the oven and pour the cooled syrup over the hot pastry. Return to the oven for 2–3 minutes, then take it out and leave to cool.

**8** Once the baklava is cool, carefully lift the individual diamond-shaped pieces out of the tin and arrange them in a serving dish.

**COOK'S TIP**
The best baklava is to be found in a busy, central pastry shop, where the wide selection of pastries on offer will also include the melt-in-the-mouth sütlü nüriye, a layered pastry filled with shaved almonds and bathed in a milky syrup; the moist, diamond-shaped şöbiyet filled with chopped pistachios; and the crunchy bülbül yuvası, a wrinkled spiral filled with nuts to resemble the nightingale's nest after which it is named.

Per portion Energy 973kcal/4059kJ; Protein 12.2g; Carbohydrate 89.9g, of which sugars 60.9g; Fat 65.2g, of which saturates 15.6g; Cholesterol 47mg; Calcium 139mg; Fibre 3.1g; Sodium 141mg.

# ROSE PETAL JAM

*THICK WITH DELICATE, SCENTED ROSE PETALS, GÜL REÇELI — ROSE PETAL JAM — IS ONE OF THE MOST TRADITIONAL OF THE TURKISH JAMS. SPOONED ON TO CHUNKS OF WARM, CRUSTY BREAD, OR OVER YOGURT, RICE PUDDING, CLOTTED CREAM, OR THIN SHEETS OF PASTRY, THE TASTE IS EXQUISITE. ANY SCENTED ROSE PETALS CAN BE USED, BUT THE PINK, COTTAGE-GARDEN ROSE IS PARTICULARLY GOOD. SOME MIDDLE EASTERN STORES SELL BAGS OF DRIED, SCENTED ROSE PETALS FOR JAM MAKING.*

MAKES ABOUT 750ML/1¼ PINTS/3 CUPS

INGREDIENTS
  450g/1lb fresh or dried scented
    rose petals
  about 350ml/12fl oz/1½ cups water
  450g/1lb/2¼ cups sugar
  juice of 1 lemon

**COOK'S TIP**
Rose petals used for culinary purposes must be sweetly scented and are generally pink or lilac in colour. In Turkey they are used to make jam and rose water, which is splashed into milk puddings and Turkish Delight, lokum.

**1** If necessary, trim and clean the petals but, if you need to rinse them, make sure they are thoroughly drained. Pour the water into a large, heavy pan. Add the rose petals and bring to the boil.

**2** Strain the petals into a bowl and return the rose-scented water to the pan. Set the strained petals aside.

**3** Add the sugar to the rose-scented water and bring it to the boil, stirring constantly. Reduce the heat and simmer for 10 minutes, or until the liquid thickens and coats the back of a wooden spoon.

**4** Stir in the lemon juice and the strained rose petals, and simmer for a further 10 minutes.

**5** Leave the mixture to cool and thicken in the pan – it should be thick and runny, requiring a spoon for serving, not a knife.

**6** Spoon the cooled jam into sterilized jars and keep in a cool, dry place for up to 6 months.

**Per batch** Energy 1886kcal/8028kJ; Protein 14.9g; Carbohydrate 477.4g, of which sugars 477g; Fat 3.6g, of which saturates 0.5g; Cholesterol 0mg; Calcium 1004mg; Fibre 9.4g; Sodium 657mg.

# SOUR CHERRY JAM

*STUNNING IN COLOUR AND TASTE, VIŞNE REÇELI IS ONE OF TURKEY'S MOST POPULAR SUMMER JAMS. WHEN THE CHERRIES ARE IN SEASON, THE PLUMP, SWEET ONES, KIRAZ, ARE PICKED TO EAT, WHEREAS THE SOUR VARIETY, VIŞNE, ARE COVETED FOR THIS JAM AND THE SUMMER BREAD PUDDING, VIŞNELI EKMEK TATLISI. AS WITH MOST TURKISH JAMS, THIS RECIPE IS FOR A RUNNY CONSERVE, WHICH NEEDS TO BE SPOONED ON TO FRESH BREAD OR DRIZZLED OVER YOGURT.*

MAKES ABOUT 2KG/4½LB

### INGREDIENTS
1kg/2¼lb/6 cups fresh sour cherries
1kg/2¼lb/5 cups sugar
juice of 1 lemon

**1** Pick over the cherries and remove the stalks. (You can remove the pits, too, if you like, but this is a laborious task and few Turkish cooks bother.)

**2** Rinse and drain the cherries and put them into a large, heavy pan. Spoon the sugar over them, making sure they are all covered, and leave the cherries to weep overnight.

**3** Place the pan over the heat and bring the liquid (there will be a substantial amount of cherry juice in the pan) to the boil, stirring from time to time.

**4** Add the lemon juice, reduce the heat, and simmer for about 25 minutes, or until the liquid thickens, bearing in mind that this will be a fairly liquid jam.

**5** Leave the jam to cool in the pan and then spoon it into sterilized jars.

**6** Keep the jam in a cool, dry place, ready to enjoy with bread, or to spoon over milk and rice puddings. The jam will keep well for up to 6 months.

### COOK'S TIPS
• Sour cherries are also boiled with sugar to make a fruit syrup, which is deep purple in colour and is used as the basis of the cool, refreshing drink, vişne suyu.
• If you do not remove the cherry stones (pits) you need to be careful when eating the jam or you could crack your teeth.

Per batch Energy 4420kcal/18840kJ; Protein 14g; Carbohydrate 1160g, of which sugars 1160g; Fat 1g, of which saturates 0g; Cholesterol 0mg; Calcium 660mg; Fibre 9g; Sodium 70mg.

# DRIED FIG JAM WITH ANISEED AND PINE NUTS

*THIS DELECTABLE HOMEMADE WINTER JAM IS MADE WITH DRIED FIGS AND PINE NUTS. IT IS FABULOUS SPREAD ON HOT, FRESH BREAD STRAIGHT FROM THE BAKER'S OVEN. LOOK FOR PLUMP, SUCCULENT DRIED FIGS WITH A SPRINGY TEXTURE — ONES THAT ARE GOOD ENOUGH TO SNACK ON — AVAILABLE IN SOME SUPERMARKETS, DELICATESSENS AND HEALTH FOOD STORES.*

MAKES ENOUGH FOR 3–4 X 450G/1LB JAM JARS

INGREDIENTS
 450g/1lb/2¼ cups sugar
 juice of 1 lemon
 5ml/1 tsp ground aniseed
 about 700g/1lb 9oz dried figs,
  coarsely chopped
 45–60ml/3–4 tbsp pine nuts

**1** Put the sugar and 600ml/1 pint/ 2½ cups water into a heavy pan and bring to the boil, stirring all the time, until the sugar has dissolved. Lower the heat and simmer for 5–10 minutes, until the syrup begins to thicken.

**2** Stir the lemon juice, aniseed and figs into the sugar syrup.

**3** Bring to the boil once more, then lower the heat again and simmer for 15–20 minutes, until the figs are tender.

**4** Add the pine nuts and simmer for a further 5 minutes. Leave the jam to cool in the pan before spooning into sterilized jars and sealing. Stored in a cool, dry place, the jam will keep for up to 6 months.

**Per jar** Energy 869kcal/3693kJ; Protein 8.4g; Carbohydrate 197.5g, of which sugars 197.5g; Fat 10.5g, of which saturates 0.5g; Cholesterol 0mg; Calcium 492mg; Fibre 13.4g; Sodium 115mg.

# PLUM TOMATO AND ALMOND JAM

*IN THE STYLE OF A CONSERVE, YOU WILL ONLY EVER COME ACROSS THIS JAM IN A TURKISH HOME, AS IT IS NOT MADE COMMERCIALLY LIKE THE WELL-KNOWN ONES MADE WITH ROSE PETALS, GREEN FIGS, SOUR CHERRIES OR QUINCE. A SUMMER JAM, MADE WITH SLIGHTLY UNRIPE OR FIRM PLUM TOMATOES, IT IS SYRUPY IN CONSISTENCY, AND SPOONED, RATHER THAN SPREAD, ON TO BREAD.*

MAKES ENOUGH FOR 2–3 X 450G/1LB
JAM JARS

INGREDIENTS
  1kg/2¼lb firm plum tomatoes
  500g/1¼ lb/2½ cups sugar
  115g/4oz/1 cup whole
    blanched almonds
  8–10 whole cloves

**1** Skin the plum tomatoes. Submerge them for a few seconds in a bowl of boiling water, then plunge them straight away into a bowl of cold water. Remove them from the water one at a time and peel off the skins with your fingers or a small knife.

**2** Place the skinned tomatoes in a heavy pan and cover with the sugar. Leave them to sit for a few hours, or overnight, to draw out some of the juices, then stir in 150ml/¼ pint/⅔ cup water. The tomatoes should be quite juicy – if not, stir in some more water, you may need up to 300ml/½ pint/ 1¼ cups.

**3** Place the pan over a low heat and stir gently with a wooden spoon until the sugar has completely dissolved.

**COOK'S TIP**
In the *güney* kitchens in the south of Turkey, plum tomatoes are often first soaked in a lime solution in order to preserve their firmness, then they are poached in a sugar syrup and served as a dessert.

**4** Bring the syrup to the boil and boil for a few minutes, skimming off any froth, then lower the heat and stir in the almonds and cloves.

**5** Simmer gently for about 25 minutes, stirring from time to time to prevent the mixture from sticking to the bottom of the pan and burning, which would spoil the flavour.

**6** Turn off the heat and leave the jam to cool in the pan before spooning into sterilized jars and sealing.

**7** Stored in a cool, dry place, the jam will keep for several months.

**Per jar** Energy 948Kcal/4016kJ; Protein 11.3g; Carbohydrate 187.1g, of which sugars 186.1g; Fat 22.4g, of which saturates 2g; Cholesterol 0mg; Calcium 204mg; Fibre 6.2g; Sodium 45mg.

# INDEX

**Picture credits:**
The publisher would like to thank Martin Brigdale for his photography throughout the book, apart from the following image (b = bottom):

iStock (Murat Sen) page 7b.